Revelation

End of Time

(Chapters 1-12)

Group Directory

Pass this Directory around and have your Group Members
fill in their names and phone numbers

Name   **Phone**

_____   _____

_____   _____

_____   _____

_____   _____

_____   _____

_____   _____

_____   _____

_____   _____

_____   _____

_____   _____

_____   _____

_____   _____

_____   _____

_____   _____

_____   _____

Revelation

EDITING AND PRODUCTION TEAM:

James F. Couch, Jr., Lyman Coleman, Sharon Penington, Cathy Tardif,
Christopher Werner, Matthew Lockhart, Erika Tiepel, Richard Peace,
Andrew Sloan, Mike Shepherd, Gregory C. Benoit,
Margaret Harris, Katharine Harris, Scott Lee

NASHVILLE, TENNESSEE

Published by Serendipity House Publishers
Nashville, Tennessee

International Standard Book Number: 1-57494-327-8

ACKNOWLEDGMENTS

Scripture quotations are taken from the Holman Christian Standard Bible,
© Copyright 2000 by Holman Bible Publishers. Used by permission.

03 04 05 06 07 08 / 10 9 8 7 6 5 4 3 2

Nashville, Tennessee
1-800-525-9563
www.serendipityhouse.com

Table of Contents

Core Values

Community: The purpose of this curriculum is to build community within the body of believers around Jesus Christ.

Group Process: To build community, the curriculum must be designed to take a group through a step-by-step process of sharing your story with one another.

Interactive Bible Study: To share your "story," the approach to Scripture in the curriculum needs to be open-ended and right brain—to "level the playing field" and encourage everyone to share.

Developmental Stages: To provide a healthy program throughout the four stages of the life cycle of a group, the curriculum needs to offer courses on three levels of commitment: (1) Beginner Level—low-level entry, high structure, to level the playing field; (2) Growth Level—deeper Bible study, flexible structure, to encourage group accountability; (3) Discipleship Level—in-depth Bible study, open structure, to move the group into high gear.

Target Audiences: To build community throughout the culture of the church, the curriculum needs to be flexible, adaptable and transferable into the structure of the average church.

Mission: To expand the Kingdom of God one person at a time by filling the "empty chair." (We add an extra chair to each group session to remind us of our mission.)

Introduction

Each healthy small group will move through various stages as it matures.

Multiply Stage: The group begins the multiplication process. Members pray about their involvement in new groups. The "new" groups begin the life cycle again with the Birth Stage.

Birth Stage: This is the time in which group members form relationships and begin to develop community. The group will spend more time in ice-breaker exercises, relational Bible study and covenant building.

Develop Stage: The inductive Bible study deepens while the group members discover and develop gifts and skills. The group explores ways to invite their neighbors and coworkers to group meetings.

Growth Stage: Here the group begins to care for one another as it learns to apply what they learn through Bible study, worship and prayer.

Subgrouping: If you have nine or more people at a meeting, Serendipity recommends you divide into subgroups of 3–6 for the Bible study. Ask one person to be the leader of each subgroup and to follow the directions for the Bible study. After 30 minutes, the Group Leader will call "time" and ask all subgroups to come together for the Caring Time.

Each group meeting should include all parts of the "three-part agenda."

 Ice-Breaker: Fun, history-giving questions are designed to warm the group and to build understanding about the other group members. You can choose to use all of the Ice-Breaker questions, especially if there is a new group member that will need help in feeling comfortable with the group.

 Bible Study: The heart of each meeting is the reading and examination of the Bible. The questions are open, discover questions that lead to further inquiry. Reference notes are provided to give everyone a "level playing field." The emphasis is on understanding what the Bible says and applying the truth to real life. The questions for each session build. There is always at least one "going deeper" question provided. You should always leave time for the last of the "questions for interaction." Should you choose, you can use the optional "going deeper" question to satisfy the desire for the challenging questions in groups that have been together for a while.

 Caring Time: All study should point us to actions. Each session ends with prayer and direction in caring for the needs of the group members. You can choose between several questions. You should always pray for the "empty chair." Who do you know that could fill that void in your group?

Sharing Your Story: These sessions are designed for members to share a little of their personal lives each time. Through a number of special techniques, each member is encouraged to move from low risk, less personal sharing to higher risk responses. This helps develop the sense of community and facilitates caregiving.

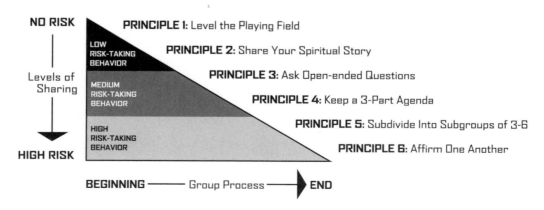

Group Covenant: A group covenant is a "contract" that spells out your expectations and the ground rules for your group. It's very important that your group discuss these issues—preferably as part of the first session.

Ground Rules:

- Priority: While you are in the group, you give the group meeting priority.

- Participation: Everyone participates and no one dominates.

- Respect: Everyone is given the right to their own opinion and all questions are encouraged and respected.

- Confidentiality: Anything that is said in the meeting is never repeated outside the meeting.

- Empty Chair: The group stays open to new people at every meeting.

- Support: Permission is given to call upon each other in time of need—even in the middle of the night.

- Advice Giving: Unsolicited advice is not allowed.

- Mission: We agree to do everything in our power to start a new group as our mission.

Issues:

- The time and place this group is going to meet is _____.

- Refreshments are _____ responsibility.

- Child care is _____ responsibility.

SESSION 1
Greetings and Doxology
SCRIPTURE REVELATION 1:1–8

Welcome

Welcome to this study of the book of Revelation, a unique book in the Bible. Revelation is the only apocalyptic book in the New Testament. Its Greek title *Apocalypsis* is a word meaning an "unveiling" or "uncovering" of future events or hidden realms, such as getting a glimpse into heaven.

Underlying both Jewish and Christian apocalyptic literature is the view that history is divided into two ages. The present age is evil and corrupt and it will be destroyed. The age to come is characterized by goodness and by God's presence and power. The central turning point in history, on which apocalyptic writers often focus, is the Day of the Lord, when the present age will give way to the new age. Christian writers understood this to be the day of Christ's return—the Second Coming.

Although the author only refers to himself as "John" (1:4), it has traditionally been accepted that he was none other than John the apostle. He wrote from the island of Patmos, a rocky island in the Aegean Sea, some ten miles long and five miles wide. He had been exiled to this tiny barren spot because of his Christian witness. Most scholars feel that the book of Revelation was written toward the end of the reign of Domitian; that is, around A.D. 90–95.

Not only is the book of Revelation unusual, it is also difficult. The world of John's Revelation is so remote from the modern world that one hardly knows where to begin in trying to understand it. Yet it is an integral part of God's Word, and therefore an important book for Christians to understand. With prayer and patience, the Holy Spirit will bring wisdom and understanding to the reader, even if specific details do not become crystal clear.

Ice-Breaker — 15 Min.

CONNECT WITH YOUR GROUP

LEADER

Be sure to read the introductory material in the front of this book prior to this first session. To help your group members get acquainted, have each person introduce him or herself and then take turns answering one or two of the Ice-Breaker questions. If time allows, you may want to discuss all three questions.

We all enjoy stories, especially ones that engage our imagination. We are about to begin a book that will do just that. First, take some time to get to know one another better by sharing your responses to the following questions.

1. What type of book or movie do you like best?

- ○ Adventure.
- ○ Science fiction.
- ○ Fantasy.
- ○ Mystery.
- ○ Historical documentary.
- ○ Other _____.

2. What vivid dream or nightmare from childhood can you still recall?

3. When have you waited and waited for someone who never showed up? What had happened that prevented him or her from meeting with you?

Bible Study — 30 Min.

READ SCRIPTURE AND DISCUSS

LEADER

Select one group member ahead of time to read aloud the Scripture passage. Then discuss the Questions for Interaction, dividing into subgroups of three to six. Be sure to allow at least 15 minutes for the Caring Time at the end.

John introduces himself to his audience, but even more importantly he introduces the true author of the book, Jesus Christ. He opens with a song of praise to the God who has redeemed us by his own blood, the God who is, and was, and is forever—the Beginning and the End. Read Revelation 1:1–8, and note God's promise to those "who hear the words of this prophecy and keep what is written in it" (v. 3).

Greetings and Doxology

1 The revelation of Jesus Christ that God gave Him to show His slaves what must quickly take place. He sent it and signified it through His angel to His slave John, ²who testified to God's word and to the testimony about Jesus Christ, in all he saw. ³Blessed is the one who reads and blessed are those who hear the words of this prophecy and keep what is written in it, because the time is near!

⁴John:

To the seven churches in the province of Asia.

Grace and peace to you from the One who is, who was, and who is coming; from the seven spirits before His throne; ⁵and from Jesus Christ, the faithful witness, the firstborn from the dead and the ruler of the kings of the earth.

To Him who loves us and has set us free from our sins by His blood, ⁶and made us a kingdom, priests to His God and Father—to Him be the glory and dominion forever and ever. Amen.

⁷Look! He is coming with the clouds,
and every eye will see Him,
including those who pierced Him.
And all the families of the earth
will mourn over Him.
This is certain. Amen.

⁸"I am the Alpha and the Omega," says the Lord God, "the One who is, who was, and who is coming, the Almighty."

Revelation 1:1–8

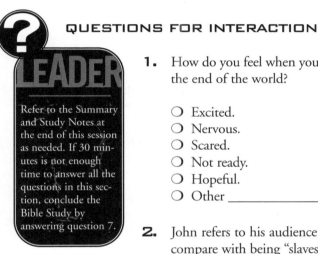

QUESTIONS FOR INTERACTION

Refer to the Summary and Study Notes at the end of this session as needed. If 30 minutes is not enough time to answer all the questions in this section, conclude the Bible Study by answering question 7.

1. How do you feel when you think about the Second Coming and the end of the world?

○ Excited.
○ Nervous.
○ Scared.
○ Not ready.
○ Hopeful.
○ Other _____.

2. John refers to his audience as "priests" in verse 6. How does this compare with being "slaves" (v. 1)? How can we be both?

3. In what ways might we be "blessed" (v. 3) as we read "the words of this prophecy"? What conditions must we meet in order to attain such blessings?

4. To what is Jesus the "faithful witness" (v. 5)? What does it mean that he is the "firstborn from the dead"?

5. What does God reveal about his character with the titles he takes in verse 8?

6. How might the expectation of Jesus' return to earth have encouraged Christians suffering persecution? How about those experiencing peace and plenty?

7. To some, Jesus is a baby or an innocent victim of crucifixion. To John, Jesus is the reigning King of Kings. How might this view of Jesus affect your day-to-day dealings with sin? With discouragement? With opposition?

GOING DEEPER:

If your group has time and/or wants a challenge, go on to this question.

8. John wrote, nearly 2,000 years ago, that the return of Christ was to "quickly take place" (v. 1). Since it has yet to occur, how do we reconcile John's statement? Does his statement that "this is certain" (v. 7) offer us hope?

Caring Time   15 Min.

APPLY THE LESSON AND PRAY FOR ONE ANOTHER

LEADER

Take some extra time in this first session to go over the introductory material at the front of this book. At the close, pass around your books and have everyone sign the Group Directory, also found in the front of this book.

This very important time is for developing and expressing your concern for each other as group members by praying for one another.

1. Agree on the group covenant and ground rules that are described in the introduction to this book.

2. How might the anticipation of Jesus' imminent return to earth affect how you live your life in the coming week?

3. Share any other prayer requests and praises, and then close in prayer. Pray specifically for God to bring someone into your life next week to fill the empty chair.

Next Week

Today we gained a small glimpse into the character of God—the Alpha and Omega, beginning and end. We were reminded that Jesus is going to return to the earth one day, perhaps this very day. In the week to come, spend time in prayer before the God who is, and was, and is to come, and consider how his imminent return might affect you if it were to happen tonight. Next week we will encounter the Son of Man, face-to-face.

Notes on Revelation 1:1–8

SUMMARY: John identifies the five stages of transmission of this book: from Father to Son to an angel to John to the reader. The prologue to the book consists of an introduction (1:1–3) stating the origin of the work, and a salutation (1:4–8) with greetings (vv. 4–5a), a doxology (vv. 5b–6), and two prophetic sayings (vv. 7–8). Even though the book has been defined as "revelation" and "prophecy," it is set in the form of a letter. In a fashion typical of Greek letters, the sender and recipients are named (v. 4) and a greeting is offered (vv. 4–5).

1:1 *The revelation.* Literally, *apokalypsis*—an unveiling or uncovering of something that was hidden; supernatural truths that could not be known had God not spoken them. This is the name that has been given to a type of literature that flourished in John's time, dealing with the details of the unseen spiritual realm and their implications for history (e.g., the book of Enoch). *of Jesus Christ.* This is not "the revelation of John" as the book is sometimes called; it is the testimony borne by Jesus Christ. He is the witness (v. 4). It was given to John. *quickly take place.* This revelation has to do with events at the end of time (as becomes clear as the book unfolds), it also deals with interpreting the meaning of events that were happening at the time of its writing in light of the expectation of the imminent return of Christ to establish his kingdom.

1:3 Since this is a book that came straight from God (as the words "revelation" and "prophecy" imply), those who read it are especially blessed. *Blessed.* This is the first of seven beatitudes in Revelation (14:13; 16:15; 19:9; 20:6; 22:7,14). To be blessed is to be in the favor of God. *reads/hear.* This probably refers to the first-century practice of reading aloud in church. *prophecy.* This is the second word that defines what kind of book this is (the first being "revelation"). Prophecy is a vision given by God of what lies ahead in both the immediate and long-term future.

1:4 *seven churches.* These seven churches are named in 1:11. There were other churches in this region, however (Acts 20:5–6; Col. 1:2; 4:13). Why only these seven are addressed is not clear. They may have been the key churches in each of seven postal regions in Asia. Certainly the number

seven was important (it represented perfection) and is used often in Revelation. The seven churches were located about 30 to 50 miles from each other on a circular road that connected them. *province of Asia.* The western half of Asia Minor (the western part of modern Turkey). *the One who is, who was, and who is coming.* A paraphrase of the name of God in Exodus 3:14–15. *the seven spirits.* This may be an unusual way of speaking about the Holy Spirit (the number seven referring to a complete manifestation of the Holy Spirit). Or it could refer to the seven archangels in Jewish tradition; or it could refer to seven angels who minister to the Lamb (4:5; 5:6).

1:5 Three titles are given to Jesus. *faithful witness.* Jesus is the one whose life made God known to the world. The Greek word for witness (*martys*) becomes "martyr" in English, and certainly in Revelation death is often the result of faithful allegiance to God (as it was for Jesus). *firstborn from the dead.* But Jesus did not remain dead; he rose again to become the sovereign Lord over the church. The title "firstborn" not only denotes priority in time, but especially stresses his right of authority over all others who are raised to life after him. *ruler of the kings.* He is also the supreme ruler of the whole earth (Phil. 2:10–11). This assertion contradicted, of course, the first-century fact that Rome ruled without rival. Domitian (who was probably emperor when John wrote) asked to be addressed as "Lord and God." But, in fact, it is Jesus who is the ruler behind rulers and will be revealed to be so at his second coming. *To Him who.* The first of several doxologies honoring Jesus (4:11; 5:9,12–13; 7:10). *by His blood.* This emphasizes the sacrificial nature of Jesus' death in terms of the Old Testament sacrificial system.

1:6 *kingdom, priests.* The early church felt itself to be the true Israel, with all the promised blessings applying to it (Gal. 3:28; Phil. 3:3; 1 Peter 2:5,9).

1:7 This combination of quotations from Daniel 7:13 and Zechariah 12:10 accents the divine identity of Jesus as God's appointed ruler of God's kingdom. The mourning is caused by the realization that judgment is coming upon those who rejected God's ruler. When Jesus returns all will see him (not just Israel); all will mourn him (as they realize that judgment is coming).

1:8 *the Alpha and the Omega.* The first and last letter in the Greek alphabet. God controls the whole sweep of history. *says the Lord God.* This is one of the two places where God speaks directly (21:5–8).

The Son of Man
SCRIPTURE REVELATION 1:9–20

Last Week

In our previous session, we were introduced to the book of Revelation and listened as John sang a song of worship to Jesus Christ. This week we will have a face-to-face encounter with Jesus, seeing him just as he appeared to John in his glorified state. This passage will also introduce us to some of the visual imagery that John uses throughout this book, as he tries to describe deep mysteries in language that common people can understand.

Ice-Breaker   15 Min.
CONNECT WITH YOUR GROUP

LEADER

Begin the session with a word of prayer. Have your group members take turns sharing their responses to one, two or all three of the Ice-Breaker questions. Be sure that everyone gets a chance to participate.

The book of Revelation uses a great deal of symbolism to describe things, and requires that we look at the world in a whole new way. Take turns sharing your thoughts and experiences with looking at life from a new perspective.

1. As a child, did you ever dress up in a costume for a program or a party? What costume do you remember as your favorite?

    ○ Angel.
    ○ Shepherd or lamb.
    ○ Pilgrim.
    ○ Indian.
    ○ Halloween spook.
    ○ Other _____.

2. How often do you remember your dreams? What bizarre dream can you still recall?

3. If you had a time machine, would you visit the past or the future? What year would you select, and why?

READ SCRIPTURE AND DISCUSS

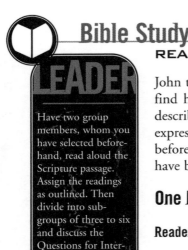

LEADER

Have two group members, whom you have selected beforehand, read aloud the Scripture passage. Assign the readings as outlined. Then divide into subgroups of three to six and discuss the Questions for Interaction.

John tells us that he is in a dream or trance-like state, and turns to find himself face-to-face with the glorified Christ. How can one describe the glory of God? John himself finds it impossible to express, so he uses symbolic images to represent the God that stands before him. Read Revelation 1:9–20, and imagine what John must have been feeling.

One Like the Son of Man

Reader One: ⁹I, John, your brother and partner in the tribulation, kingdom, and perseverance in Jesus, was on the island called Patmos because of God's word and the testimony about Jesus. ¹⁰I was in the Spirit on the Lord's day, and I heard behind me a loud voice like a trumpet ¹¹saying, "Write on a scroll what you see and send it to the seven churches: Ephesus, Smyrna, Pergamum, Thyatira, Sardis, Philadelphia, and Laodicea."

Reader Two: ¹²I turned to see the voice that was speaking to me. When I turned I saw seven gold lampstands, ¹³and among the lampstands was One like the Son of Man, dressed in a long robe, and with a gold sash wrapped around His chest. ¹⁴His head and hair were white like wool—white as snow, His eyes like a fiery flame, ¹⁵His feet like fine bronze fired in a furnace, and His voice like the sound of cascading waters. ¹⁶In His right hand He had seven stars; from His mouth came a sharp two-edged sword; and His face was shining like the sun at midday.

Reader One: ¹⁷When I saw Him, I fell at His feet like a dead man. He laid His right hand on me, and said,

Reader Two: "Don't be afraid! I am the First and the Last, ¹⁸and the Living One. I was dead, but look—I am alive forever and ever, and I hold the keys of death and Hades. ¹⁹Therefore write what you have seen, what is, and what will take place after this. ²⁰The secret of the seven stars you saw in My right hand, and of the seven gold lampstands, is this: the seven stars are the angels of the seven churches, and the seven lamp stands are the seven churches.

Revelation 1:9–20

QUESTIONS FOR INTERACTION

LEADER

Refer to the Summary and Study Notes at the end of this session as needed. If 30 minutes is not enough time to answer all of the questions in this section, conclude the Bible Study by answering question 7.

1. What "tribulations" have you faced in your life?

- ○ Sickness.
- ○ Abandonment by friends.
- ○ False accusations.
- ○ Punishment for something I did wrong.
- ○ Never being good enough to be chosen for a team.
- ○ Persecution for being a Christian.
- ○ Other _____.

2. What do the seven lampstands and seven stars represent? Why are these images used?

3. Discuss the physical appearance of Christ in this passage. Remember that much of this book's visual imagery is symbolic, not necessarily literal. What does Jesus' appearance suggest of his character?

4. Why is there a "sharp two-edged sword" coming from Jesus' mouth (v. 16)? What does this represent (compare Heb. 4:12)?

5. Jesus says, "I am the First and the Last, and the Living One. I was dead, but look—I am alive forever and ever" (vv. 17–18). Compare this with 1:8. What does this tell us about the person of Jesus Christ?

6. If you turned and saw "One like the Son of Man" standing behind you, looking like what John describes, how would you react?

- ○ Faint dead away.
- ○ Run.
- ○ Rejoice and sing praises.
- ○ Shake his hand.
- ○ Other _____.

7. Why does Jesus say, "Don't be afraid" (v. 17)? How does this make you feel about God and your relationship with him?

GOING DEEPER:

If your group has time and/or wants a challenge, go on to this question.

8. John calls himself our "partner in the tribulation, kingdom, and perseverance" (v. 9). This "tribulation" might refer to the Great Tribulation, to be discussed later, or to present tribulations, such as John's exile to Patmos. Why does he link together the concepts of tribulation, God's kingdom and perseverance?

Caring Time   15 Min.

APPLY THE LESSON AND PRAY FOR ONE ANOTHER

LEADER

Bring the group together for the Caring Time. Begin by sharing responses to all three questions. Then share prayer requests and close in a group prayer. Those who do not feel comfortable praying aloud should not feel pressured to do so. As the leader, conclude the prayer time and be sure to pray for the empty chair.

John met God face-to-face, and one day each one of us will, as well. It is vital that we be prepared for that meeting, finding forgiveness and salvation through the blood of Jesus Christ. Take some time now to discuss the Gospel of God's salvation, and to support any who are undergoing trials or tribulation.

1. Do you have a personal relationship with Jesus Christ? Do you acknowledge him as God and Savior?

2. Are you undergoing any tribulations at present? How can the group help?

3. Do you know someone who needs to know Jesus? Can you invite that person next week?

P.S. *Add new group members to the Group Directory at the front of this book.*

Next Week

Today we met the living God, and found that he is not quite as he is usually pictured in art or popular culture. In the coming week, consider whether you are prepared yourself to meet God face-to-face; if not, ask for God's forgiveness and salvation through the death and resurrection of Jesus Christ. If you know someone else who needs God's forgiveness, pray for God to help you in reaching out to that person. Next week we will read a letter that God writes to some of the churches that were meeting in Asia in John's day.

Notes on Revelation 1:9–20

SUMMARY: The first vision (1:9–3:22) begins with John's account of his vision of the exalted Christ, during which he receives his commission to write this book. A series of divine attributes are ascribed to Christ. They convey the sense of an otherworldly visitor who possessed great power, wisdom and authority (Dan. 7:9). The threefold statement in verse 19 can be taken as the outline of the book of Revelation. John is to write what he had seen (i.e. the vision of the Son of Man; vv. 9–20), what was then and there the state of the church (which he will do in chapters 2 and 3 through the seven letters to seven churches), and what is yet to come (which comprises the rest of the book).

1:9 John writes as one who has paid the price of being a Christian, following the example of his Lord. Thus he knows exactly what his readers are going through. *tribulation.* The tribulation that comes from being a Christian (John 16:33) will intensify during the last days before the full establishment of God's kingdom. *Patmos.* A small island in the Aegean Sea off the coast of modern Turkey; probably a Roman penal colony.

1:10 *in the Spirit.* A trance, an ecstatic experience; a type of mystical experience (Acts 10:10; 11:5; 22:17; 2 Cor. 12:2–4). *the Lord's day.* The first day of the week (Sunday) when Christians met to worship together because it was on this day that Jesus rose from the dead.

1:11 The churches are named in geographical order as one went around the circular road on which they were located. *Write on a scroll.* It is John's job to translate this vision into a written manuscript. As he does so, he will quite naturally draw upon those words, phrases and pictures that are a part of his background. This will include abundant Old Testament imagery.

1:12 *seven gold lampstands.* These stand for the seven churches (v. 20). They are a fitting symbol for the church, which is meant to be a light to the world (Matt. 5:14–16).

1:13 *One like the Son of Man.* This phrase is from Daniel 7:13. It is a rather vague title (it could mean simply "a human being"), but it was more likely a messianic description. Jesus used it for himself, filling it with new meaning and content (Mark 8:31–10:45). It became Jesus' most com-

mon title for himself. *dressed in a long robe.* Jesus wore the full-length robe of a high priest. In 1:1–20, Jesus is presented in the threefold office of prophet (v. 1), priest (v. 13), and king (v. 5).

1:16 *sword.* The sword that issues from the mouth of Jesus represents the fact of divine judgment (2:16; 19:15,21; Isa. 49:2; Heb. 4:12). *His face was shining like the sun.* The shimmering glory of Jesus recalls the parallel experience on the Mount of Transfiguration (Matt. 17:2).

1:17 John's response to this glorious vision of Jesus is like the response of Old Testament prophets in similar circumstances (Josh. 5:14; Isa. 6:5; Ezek. 1:28; Dan. 8:17; 10:15). *laid His right hand on me.* Jesus thus commissions John to undertake the task of writing what he has seen in this vision (v.19). *Don't be afraid.* Just as John's response parallels that of the Old Testament prophets who glimpsed God's glory, so these words from Jesus parallel those that God spoke to these same Old Testament prophets. These words from Jesus would have been familiar to John. He heard them on the Sea of Galilee (Matt. 14:27) and at the Mount of Transfiguration (Matt. 17:7). *the First and the Last.* This is parallel to the phrase "the Alpha and the Omega," spoken by God (1:8).

1:18 *the Living One.* This parallels the Old Testament title for God as "The Living God," that is, the God who acts in contrast to the idols (Josh. 3:10; Ps. 42:2; 84:2). Likewise, Jesus possesses life itself (John 1:4) in contrast to the dead gods that populated the imagination of people in the Roman world. His resurrection is a stark demonstration of this quality. *the keys.* Jesus' possession of these keys means that he has the power and the authority to unlock death and Hades (which Jews viewed as the resting place for the dead prior to the final judgment) and lead the dead into Life itself.

1:20 *lampstands.* Moses too had a vision of seven lampstands that he was to build for the tabernacle. He combined these into a single lamp, whereas John saw seven separate lamps.

Letters to the Churches, Part 1

SCRIPTURE REVELATION 2:1–29

Last Week

In last week's session, we saw John faint with fear as he was overwhelmed by his face-to-face meeting with God. We were reminded not to be afraid and to have hope in the trials of life. This week God himself will dictate some letters that will be sent to Christians living in Asia under Roman rule. We will learn that one of the things God prizes most is the willingness of his people to endure.

Ice-Breaker   15 Min.

CONNECT WITH YOUR GROUP

LEADER

Choose one or two of the Ice-Breaker questions. If you have a new group member you may want to do all three. Remember to stick closely to the three-part agenda and the time allowed for each segment.

Childhood brings back a mix of memories for most of us—tests in school, our first time falling in love, playing with friends and so much more. Share some of your own memories from those times.

1. What type of tests were you best at in high school? Worst at?

2. Who was your best friend in grade school? Where is that person now?

3. At what sport or contest have you been the victor?

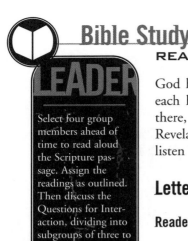

READ SCRIPTURE AND DISCUSS

God himself sends letters out to four of the churches in Asia. In each he commends them for the good things that he has found there, but also warns them of things they need to improve. Read Revelation 2:1–29, and note the blessings that come to those who listen to the Holy Spirit.

Letters to Four Churches

Reader One: 2 "To the angel of the church in Ephesus write:

"The One who holds the seven stars in His right hand and who walks among the seven gold lampstands says: ²I know your works, your labor, and your endurance, and that you cannot tolerate evil. You have tested those who call themselves apostles and are not, and you have found them to be liars. ³You also possess endurance and have tolerated many things because of My name, and have not grown weary. ⁴But I have this against you: you have abandoned the love you had at first. ⁵Remember then how far you have fallen; repent, and do the works you did at first. Otherwise, I will come to you and remove your lampstand from its place—unless you repent. ⁶Yet you do have this: you hate the practices of the Nicolaitans, which I also hate.

⁷"Anyone who has an ear should listen to what the Spirit says to the churches. I will give the victor the right to eat from the tree of life, which is in the paradise of God.

Reader Two: ⁸"To the angel of the church in Smyrna write:

"The First and the Last, the One who was dead and came to life, says: ⁹I know your tribulation and poverty, yet you are rich. I know the slander of those who say they are Jews and are not, but are a synagogue of Satan. ¹⁰Don't be afraid of what you are about to suffer. Look, the Devil is about to throw some of you into prison to test you, and you will have tribulation for 10 days. Be faithful until death, and I will give you the crown of life.

¹¹"Anyone who has an ear should listen to what the Spirit says to the churches. The victor will never be harmed by the second death.

Reader Three: ¹²"To the angel of the church in Pergamum write:

"The One who has the sharp, two-edged sword says: ¹³I know where you live—where Satan's throne is! And you are holding on to My name and did not deny your faith in Me, even in the days of Antipas, My faithful witness, who was killed among you, where Satan lives. ¹⁴But I have a few things against you. You have some there who hold to the teaching of Balaam, who taught Balak to place a stumbling block in front of the sons of Israel: to eat meat sacrificed to idols and to commit sexual immorality. ¹⁵In the same way, you also have those who hold to the teaching of the Nicolaitans. ¹⁶Therefore repent! Otherwise, I will come to you quickly and fight against them with the sword of My mouth.

¹⁷"Anyone who has an ear should listen to what the Spirit says to the churches. I will give the victor some of the hidden manna. I will also give him a white stone, and on the stone a new name is inscribed that no one knows except the one who receives it.

Reader Four: ¹⁸"To the angel of the church in Thyatira write:

"The Son of God, the One whose eyes are like a fiery flame, and whose feet are like fine bronze says: ¹⁹I know your works—your love, faithfulness, service, and endurance. Your last works are greater than the first. ²⁰But I have this against you: you tolerate the woman Jezebel, who calls herself a prophetess, and teaches and deceives My slaves to commit sexual immorality and to eat meat sacrificed to idols. ²¹I gave her time to repent, but she does not want to repent of her sexual immorality. ²²Look! I will throw her into a sickbed, and those who commit adultery with her into great tribulation, unless they repent of her practices. ²³I will kill her children with the plague. Then all the churches will know that I am the One who examines minds and hearts, and I will give to each of you according to your works. ²⁴I say to the rest of you in Thyatira, who do not hold this teaching, who haven't known the deep things of Satan—as they say—I do not put any other burden on you. ²⁵But hold on to what you have until I come. ²⁶The victor and the one who keeps My works to the end: I will give him authority over the nations—

²⁷and He will shepherd them with an iron scepter;
He will shatter them like pottery—

just as I have received this from My Father. ²⁸I will also give him the morning star. ²⁹"Anyone who has an ear should listen to what the Spirit says to the churches.

Revelation 2:1–29

QUESTIONS FOR INTERACTION

Refer to the Summary and Study Notes at the end of this session as needed. If 30 minutes is not enough time to answer all of the questions in this section, conclude the Bible Study by answering question 7.

1. Note that each of these churches is praised by God for their endurance. What does this suggest about what it means to follow Christ?

2. What does it mean that the members of the church at Ephesus "have abandoned the love you had at first" (v. 4)? Why is this so bad that God would threaten to "remove their lampstand" (v. 5)?

3. Who is the "victor" that God refers to so often (vv. 7,11,17,26)? What rewards will the victor receive?

4. What do Jesus' words to the church in Smyrna, in verses 8–11, teach about suffering?

5. In verses 12–17, how are the Christians in Pergamum being tested? Which do you think is easier to endure: Persecution by enemies or seduction by the culture, and why?

6. Sexual immorality was a problem for the early church (vv. 20–22). How does the church today still face this problem?

7. Have you lost your first love for Christ (v. 4)? What can help you in the coming week to keep that love alive?

GOING DEEPER:

If your group has time and/or wants a challenge, go on to this question.

8. The Nicolaitans were probably a group that tried to mix Christian theology with worldly practices and ideas. The "teaching of Balaam" (v. 14) and the "woman Jezebel" (v. 20) also refer to those who were trying to blend Christianity with paganism. How does this happen in the church today?

Caring Time   15 Min.

APPLY THE LESSON AND PRAY FOR ONE ANOTHER

LEADER

Begin the Caring Time by having group members take turns sharing responses to all three questions. Be sure to save at least the last five minutes for a time of group prayer. Remember to include a prayer for the empty chair when concluding the prayer time.

The teachings of the world are constantly competing with those of Jesus Christ. One common area of compromise is that of sexual purity. Another, more subtle area is in the world's teachings on love, notably "love yourself first." Take some time now to build up one another with sharing and prayer so that we can have the strength to resist compromising our values.

1. How is this group doing at keeping the love of Christ alive? At loving one another?

2. What can you do to keep sexually pure? How can the group pray for you?

3. What worldly teachings, ideas or priorities are competing with Christ in your life?

Next Week

Today we were challenged with the fact that God will not tolerate any adulteration of his Gospel, whether with worldly teachings or even just the tendency to let our love grow cold. We also were comforted in knowing that God examines minds and hearts, and he is pleased by our efforts to endure in the face of trials or temptation. In the coming week, prayerfully examine your own life for areas of compromise, and ask God to strengthen you to endure. Next week we will read more of the letters that God wrote to the churches in Asia.

Notes on Revelation 2:1–29

SUMMARY: The second part of this first vision consists of seven letters to the seven churches that are the focus of this letter. The letters are similar in form. Each is prefaced with a word to the angel of the church; each then begins with a descriptive phrase about Christ chosen from the titles of Jesus in the opening vision (1:13–18); each passes judgment on the church. The aim of these seven letters is to impress upon the church as a whole the need for endurance in the face of the coming persecution.

2:1 *the church in Ephesus.* More is known about this church than any other in the first century. One of Paul's letters is addressed to it; this church is the focus of 1 and 2 Timothy; and is addressed by John in his first epistle. *the seven stars/the seven gold lampstands.* In each case, the phrase chosen is appropriate for the church in view. Here Jesus is the one who holds control over the seven angels and he walks among the seven churches. He has come to inspect his church.

2:2 *your labor/your endurance.* These words define the nature of the "deeds" noted by Christ in his inspection of the church. "Endurance" can be translated as "patience," and refers to their willingness to endure the hostile reactions of those around them. *tested those.* They did not reject out of hand those who came to them. They "tested the spirits" (as John had urged them in 1 John 4:1) and found these false apostles wanting. They are commended for their willingness to maintain their orthodoxy. *call themselves apostles.* In 1 Timothy, Paul dealt with the problem of false teachers in the Ephesian church (Acts 20:29). Apparently the church had taken his words to heart and rid themselves of these errant individuals.

2:6 *Nicolaitans.* It is hard to say for certain who these individuals are. They are some sort of heretical sect who mixed Christianity and pagan practices such as idolatry and immorality.

2:7 *churches.* The plural is significant. These words are not intended only for the church at Ephesus, but as a challenge to all churches. *tree of life.* See 22:2,14 and Genesis 2:9; 3:22–24. *paradise.* This was originally a Persian word for a garden of great delight.

2:8 *Smyrna.* A beautiful city some 35 miles north of Ephesus on the eastern shore of the Aegean Sea. *the First and the Last.* Smyrna had strong ties to Rome. The imperial cult, with its emperor worship, was strong there. It is not surprising therefore that Jesus reminds them that he alone is sovereign. *was dead and came to life.* His second title assures them that they too can overcome death, an important promise given the persecution they faced.

2:9 *tribulation.* This is a church under siege. *rich.* Though they are experiencing material poverty, they are rich spiritually (Matt. 5:11–12).

2:11 *second death.* The death of the wicked in eternity.

2:12 *Pergamum.* Located some 40 miles north of Smyrna and 10 miles inland from the Aegean Sea, the city sat atop a thousand-foot high cone-shaped hill. It was the site of a famous library.

2:13 *I know where you live.* Jesus is well aware of how difficult it is to be a Christian in the city of Pergamum. *where Satan's throne is.* Pagan religion flourished in Pergamum.

2:14 *Balaam.* The reference is to the Old Testament story in which Balaam advised the Moabite women to seduce the Israelites into leaving their God (Num. 25:1–3; 31:16).

2:17 *hidden manna.* Manna was the supernatural food given to the Israelites during their wanderings in the wilderness. *white stone.* It is by no means clear what this refers to. It might refer to the white stone which gave admission to a banquet, with the allusion here being to the messianic banquet and the manna.

2:18 *Thyatira.* The city of Thyatira was southeast of Pergamum. It was a manufacturing and marketing center, with numerous trade guilds. Lydia, the seller of purple, was from Thyatira (Acts 16:14). *Son of God.* By his title, Jesus reminds the church that he alone is the true Son of God.

2:20 *tolerate.* Even though the church was growing in love and service, they allowed false teaching to exist. Unlike the Ephesians, who tested the teachers and rejected those who were false, those in Thyatira refused to deal with the matter of Jezebel. *Jezebel.* The original Jezebel was the wicked wife of Israel's King Ahab who promoted the detestable worship of Baal (1 Kin. 16:29–33; 2 Kin. 9:30–37). Her first-century counterpart played the same role in the church; i.e., the promotion of false practices. *prophetess.* Prophecy was highly valued in the New Testament church. While it included the idea of predicting the future (Acts 11:27–28), it mainly involved the application of God's truth. Jezebel claimed to be this kind of inspired teacher and some in the church followed her.

2:24 *the deep things of Satan.* She claimed to lead people into the deep things of God, but was actually introducing them to the mysteries of Satan.

2:28 *the morning star.* There is no clear understanding about what this refers to. Suggestions include: Jesus himself, the Holy Spirit, and immortality (Dan. 12:3).

SESSION 4
Letters to the Churches, Part 2
SCRIPTURE REVELATION 3:1–22

Last Week

In our previous session, we read some letters that God himself sent to Christians living in Asia. We were reminded not to let worldly teachings and values compromise our beliefs and make our love for Jesus grow cold. This week we will read some more letters from God, in which he will state clearly what sorts of behavior and practices displease him and even make him ill.

Ice-Breaker   15 Min.

CONNECT WITH YOUR GROUP

LEADER

Open the session with a word of prayer, and then welcome and introduce new group members. Choose one, two or all three of the Ice-Breaker questions.

We are all enamored from time to time with famous people, whether they are athletes, celebrities, politicians or from some other area of renown. Take turns sharing your thoughts about characteristics and people you admire.

1. If you could have one of these reputations, which would you choose?

    ○ Star athlete.
    ○ Famous celebrity.
    ○ Brilliant scientist.
    ○ Great artist.
    ○ A person devoted entirely to God.
    ○ Other _____.

2. Did you ever receive credit for something that you didn't do? How did you feel?

3. If you could have dinner with any contemporary famous person, whom would you choose?

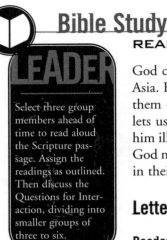

Bible Study

READ SCRIPTURE AND DISCUSS

LEADER

Select three group members ahead of time to read aloud the Scripture passage. Assign the readings as outlined. Then discuss the Questions for Interaction, dividing into smaller groups of three to six.

God continues writing letters, this time to three more churches in Asia. He is very frank with the Christians in these churches, telling them exactly what pleases him and what displeases him. He even lets us know that sometimes our behavior and attitudes can make him ill. Read Revelation 3:1–22, and note that what seems to please God most is a sincere willingness on the part of his people to endure in their obedience and love for him.

Letters to Three Churches

Reader One: 3 "To the angel of the church in Sardis write:

"The One who has the seven spirits of God and the seven stars says: I know your works; you have a reputation for being alive, but you are dead. ²Be alert and strengthen what remains, which is about to die, for I have not found your works complete before My God. ³Remember therefore what you have received and heard; keep it, and repent. But if you are not alert, I will come like a thief, and you have no idea at what hour I will come against you. ⁴But you have a few people in Sardis who have not defiled their clothes, and they will walk with Me in white, because they are worthy. ⁵In the same way, the victor will be dressed in white clothes, and I will never erase his name from the book of life, but will acknowledge his name before My Father and before His angels.

⁶"Anyone who has an ear should listen to what the Spirit says to the churches.

Reader Two: ⁷"To the angel of the church in Philadelphia write:

"The Holy One, the True One, the One who has the key of David, who opens and no one will close, and closes and no one opens says: ⁸I know your works. Because you have limited strength, have kept My word, and have not denied My name, look, I have placed before you an open door that no one is able to close. ⁹Take note! I will make those from the synagogue of Satan, who claim to be Jews and are not, but are lying—note this—I will make them come and bow down at your feet, and they will know that I have loved you. ¹⁰Because you have kept My command to endure, I will also keep you from the hour of testing that is going to come over the whole world to test those who live on the earth. ¹¹I am coming quickly. Hold on to what you have, so that no one takes your crown. ¹²The victor: I will make him a pillar in the sanctuary of My God, and he will never go out again. I will write on him the name of My God, and the name of the city of My God—the new Jerusalem, which comes down out of heaven from My God—and My new name.

¹³"Anyone who has an ear should listen to what the Spirit says to the churches.

Reader Three: ¹⁴"To the angel of the church in Laodicea write:

"The Amen, the faithful and true Witness, the Originator of God's creation says: ¹⁵I know your works, that you are neither cold nor hot. I wish that you were cold or hot. ¹⁶So, because you are lukewarm, and neither hot nor cold, I am going to vomit you out of My mouth. ¹⁷Because you say, 'I'm rich; I have become wealthy, and need nothing,' and you don't know that you are wretched, pitiful, poor, blind, and naked, ¹⁸I advise you to buy from Me gold refined in the fire so that you may be rich, and white clothes so that you may be dressed and your shameful nakedness not be exposed, and ointment to spread on your eyes so that you may see. ¹⁹As many as I love, I rebuke and discipline. So be committed and repent. ²⁰Listen! I stand at the door and knock. If anyone hears My voice and opens the door, I will come in to him and have dinner with him, and he with Me. ²¹The victor: I will give him the right to sit with Me on My throne, just as I also won the victory and sat down with My Father on His throne.

²²"Anyone who has an ear should listen to what the Spirit says to the churches."

Revelation 3:1–22

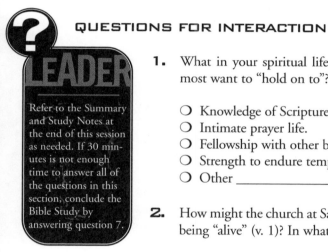

QUESTIONS FOR INTERACTION

Refer to the Summary and Study Notes at the end of this session as needed. If 30 minutes is not enough time to answer all of the questions in this section, conclude the Bible Study by answering question 7.

1. What in your spiritual life is most valuable to you, which you most want to "hold on to"?

- ○ Knowledge of Scripture.
- ○ Intimate prayer life.
- ○ Fellowship with other believers.
- ○ Strength to endure temptation.
- ○ Other _____.

2. How might the church at Sardis have maintained a reputation for being "alive" (v. 1)? In what way had it actually died?

3. What does it mean that the church at Sardis needed to "strengthen what remains" (v. 2)? How would being "alert" help in this strengthening?

4. The church at Philadelphia receives no rebuke in these letters from God. What was it that so pleased God about this church?

5. What does it mean to be "neither cold nor hot" (v. 15)? Why is this so repulsive to God?

6. What does Jesus tell the Laodicean church to do in verse 18? How will you pursue true wealth in your own life?

7. What is Jesus waiting for at the door of your life right now (v. 20)? What room in your life is not open to Jesus?

GOING DEEPER:

If your group has time and/or wants a challenge, go on to this question.

8. Even the church of Philadelphia is warned that they must "hold on to what you have, so that no one takes your crown" (v. 11). What are they to hold on to? What does it mean to lose their crown?

Caring Time   15 Min.

APPLY THE LESSON AND PRAY FOR ONE ANOTHER

LEADER

Be sure to save at least 15 minutes for this important time. After sharing responses to all three questions and asking for prayer requests, close in a time of group prayer.

It is easy to become complacent in our walk with God, especially if we have a reputation for being godly. Spend some time together confessing areas where you may be slipping into a lukewarm faith, and prayerfully seek to strengthen one another.

1. Are you hot, cold or lukewarm in your relationship with God at present? What do you need to get heated up?

2. How accurate is your reputation? Are you living out your beliefs, or just maintaining an image?

3. Have you been struggling lately to keep God's word in some area of your life? How can this group help?

Next Week

This week we learned that God, who sees our hearts and minds, also knows whether our faith is really hot or just lukewarm. In the coming week, ask God to strengthen your heart so you can stay "on fire" for Jesus, showing you areas in your own life where you are losing the flame of your first love. Next week we will be taken into the actual throne room of God himself.

SUMMARY: The remaining three churches are now addressed. Sardis had once been a powerful city, but by the first century it had lost much of its influence. Like the church at Smyrna (2:8–11), the church at Philadelphia gets unqualified praise. The letters to these two churches are quite similar in content. John identifies the threefold reward for faithfulness: vindication before their enemies, deliverance from the coming worldwide trials and a secure place in the coming age. The last city is Laodicea. Like the church at Sardis, this church seems to be prosperous and without persecution or heresy. The call to repentance in the last few verses in this passage indicates that the church is not beyond recovery.

3:1 *Sardis.* The temple in Sardis was dedicated to the goddess Cybele who was thought to have the power to bring dead people back to life. *reputation for being alive.* The church at Sardis was thought to be vital and full of life, but in fact it was spiritually dead.

3:2 *Be alert.* This is the first of five commands. This particular command means "be watchful" and may refer, in the historical context, to the fact that, despite the nearly perpendicular walls of the citadel, the town had fallen twice to its enemies due to a lack of watchfulness. *I have not found your works complete.* Unlike the other churches addressed thus far, apparently this church was not troubled by persecution nor was heresy an issue.

3:4 *walk with Me in white.* The image of white garments is used elsewhere in Revelation: the Laodiceans are told to buy white garments to cover their nakedness (3:18); the 24 elders have white garments (4:4); the martyrs are given white robes (6:11); a great crowd stands before God dressed in white garments washed in the blood of the Lamb (7:9,13); the army of heaven is dressed in white (19:14). White garments are, apparently, the dress of heaven.

3:5 *book of life.* The image is of some sort of divine ledger in which the names of the people are written. This picture was first found in the Old Testament (Ex. 32:32–33; Ps. 69:28; Dan. 12:1).

3:7 *Philadelphia.* This was the newest of the seven cities. It was located 28 miles southeast of Sardis in a region of severe earthquakes. *The Holy One, the True One.* Both names were titles for God. *the key*

of David. A symbolic way of speaking about the one who controls access to the royal house; in this case, the messianic kingdom (Isa. 22:22).

3:8 *limited strength.* The congregation is apparently small and without much impact on the city. *have kept My Word.* Yet in the recent persecution, they did not deny Jesus.

3:9 *the synagogue of Satan.* There has been conflict between the church and synagogue at Philadelphia, probably over the question of who were the people of God. One day those of the synagogue will acknowledge that the church is loved by God.

3:10 *hour of testing.* The church at Philadelphia will have to face persecution by Rome. They are promised that Christ will shield them during this terrible period. This phrase also looks ahead to the tribulation and testing that will precede the establishment of Christ's kingdom on earth at the Second Coming (13:5–10; Dan. 12:1; Mark 13:14–19; 2 Thess. 2:1–12).

3:11 *I am coming quickly.* The coming of Christ to Ephesus (2:5), Pergamum (2:16) and Sardis (3:3) would be in judgment of some sort. However, his coming to Philadelphia will be a great joy, in that this will signal the end of tribulation and the beginning of life in his kingdom.

3:12 *a pillar.* This metaphor speaks of stability and permanence (Gal. 2:9; 1 Tim. 3:15).

3:14 *Laodicea.* A wealthy city, situated at the intersection of three major roads, known for its banking and industry. Paul wrote a letter to this church which, unfortunately, has been lost (Col. 4:16). *the faithful and true Witness.* This amplifies the meaning of the previous title. Jesus is, indeed, the one who testifies to that which is true.

3:15 *neither cold nor hot.* Laodicea was located near both Hierapolis (which had hot springs with mineral-laden water thought to promote healing) and Colosse (which had streams of cold, pure water).

3:16 *lukewarm.* By the time the hot water got to Laodicea from the springs at Hierapolis six miles away, it was tepid. *vomit you out of My mouth.* Lukewarm, mineral-filled water was probably so foul-tasting that one would be tempted to spit it out.

3:17 *I have become wealthy.* This image would be meaningful in this city with a thriving banking system. The church was affluent and without a sense of need. *poor, blind, and naked.* This picture of the church stands in sharp contrast to the everyday world of Laodicea, which was known for its wealth, its eye salve and its luxurious clothing.

3:18 *gold.* Thinking themselves "rich" (v. 17), they will become truly rich only with the spiritual gold they can get from Christ.

3:19 *love.* The Greek word used here is *phileo,* which is the kind of warm and tender affection one feels toward family members. *repent.* Once again, the call is to repentance (2:5,16; 3:3). They must turn away from their lukewarmness.

3:20 *have dinner with him.* Sharing a meal was a sign that a bond existed between people. It was a symbol of affection, of confidence, of intimacy.

The Throne in Heaven
SCRIPTURE REVELATION 4:1–11

Last Week

We had the privilege last week of reading more of the letters that God wrote to some of the churches in Asia. Through those letters, God warned us that he will not tolerate a lukewarm faith. He also reminded us that true wealth is only found through him and not through the world. This week we will gain another incredible privilege—we will ascend into heaven and stand before the very throne of God.

Ice-Breaker   15 Min.

CONNECT WITH YOUR GROUP

LEADER

Open with a word of prayer, and then introduce any new people or visitors. If you have a new group member today, remember to do all three Ice-Breaker questions to help him or her get acquainted with everyone.

There are times when we see things that take our breath away, that stay in our memories for the rest of our lives. They may be as simple as a glorious sunset or a lovely bride, or they may be rare and unique events. Take turns sharing some of your unique memories.

1. What interesting animals have you seen in the wild? (Zoos don't count.)

○ Eagle.
○ Buffalo.
○ Lion.
○ Bear.
○ Owl.
○ Elephant.
○ Alligator.
○ Other _____.

2. Where have you seen the most spectacular sunset?

3. What is the biggest church, palace or castle you've ever been in? How did you feel while inside?

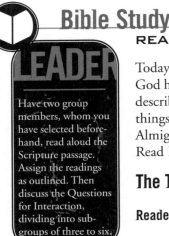

LEADER

Have two group members, whom you have selected beforehand, read aloud the Scripture passage. Assign the readings as outlined. Then discuss the Questions for Interaction, dividing into subgroups of three to six.

Today we will have the privilege of entering the throne room of God himself. The One seated there defies description. How can one describe the "great God of wonders" who created and sustains all things? One thing does become clear from John's description—the Almighty God is majestic, powerful and worthy of all our praise. Read Revelation 4:1–11, and note how God is worshiped.

The Throne in Heaven

Reader One: 4 After this I looked, and there in heaven was an open door. The first voice that I had heard speaking to me like a trumpet said,

Reader Two: "Come up here, and I will show you what must take place after this."

Reader One: ²Immediately I was in the Spirit, and there in heaven a throne was set. One was seated on the throne, ³and the One seated looked like jasper and carnelian stone. A rainbow that looked like an emerald surrounded the throne. ⁴Around that throne were 24 thrones, and on the thrones sat 24 elders dressed in white clothes, with gold crowns on their heads. ⁵From the throne came flashes of lightning, rumblings, and thunder. Burning before the throne were seven fiery torches, which are the seven spirits of God. ⁶Also before the throne was something like a sea of glass, similar to crystal. In the middle and around the throne were four living creatures covered with eyes in front and in back. ⁷The first living creature was like a lion; the second living creature was like a calf; the third living creature had a face like a man; and the fourth living creature was like a flying eagle. ⁸Each of the four living creatures had six wings; they were covered with eyes around and inside. Day and night they never stop, saying:

Reader Two: Holy, holy, holy,
Lord God, the Almighty,
who was, who is, and who is coming.

Reader One: ⁹Whenever the living creatures give glory, honor, and thanks to the One seated on the throne, the One who lives forever and ever, ¹⁰the 24 elders fall down before the One seated on the throne, worship the One who lives forever and ever, cast their crowns before the throne, and say:

Reader Two: ¹¹ Our Lord and God,
You are worthy to receive
glory and honor and power,
because You have created all things,
and because of Your will
they exist and were created.

Revelation 4:1–11

QUESTIONS FOR INTERACTION

LEADER

Refer to the Summary and Study Notes at the end of this session as needed. If 30 minutes is not enough time to answer all of the questions in this section, conclude the Bible Study by answering question 7.

1. How accessible does God seem to you right now?

○ Open door policy.
○ He's there if I need him.
○ I'm not sure how to get a hold of him.
○ Don't call me, I'll call you.
○ Other _____.

2. The first thing John sees of heaven is an open door. What does this suggest about heaven? About God's relationship with humanity?

3. The "seven spirits of God," probably a reference to the Holy Spirit, are portrayed as "fiery torches" (v. 5). Why is this image used of the Spirit of God?

4. What do the white robes and gold crowns of the 24 elders suggest?

5. Why do the 24 elders "cast their crowns before the throne" (v. 10)?

6. What one word would you use to describe God as he is revealed here?

○ Majestic.
○ Incomprehensible.
○ Terrifying.
○ All-powerful.
○ Other _____.

7. When you approach God in prayer, what is your customary attitude?

○ Confident.
○ Casual.
○ Fearful.
○ Humble.
○ Bold.
○ Other _____.

How might the description of God in today's passage affect your attitude?

GOING DEEPER:

If your group has time and/or wants a challenge, go on to this question.

8. The imagery of God's throne in this passage suggests that he is incomprehensible, "past finding out" (Rom. 11:33, KJV). How are we to reconcile God's "open door" availability with this power and majesty?

Caring Time   15 Min.

APPLY THE LESSON AND PRAY FOR ONE ANOTHER

LEADER

Encourage everyone to participate in this important time and be sure that each group member is receiving prayer support. Continue to pray for the empty chair in the closing group prayer.

Comfort and encourage one another with this time of sharing and prayer. Begin by sharing your responses to the following questions. Be sure to offer any other prayer requests and concerns before closing in prayer.

1. Share with the group a spiritual struggle or victory from this past week.

2. What concern do you need to take before the awe-inspiring throne of God?

3. How do you feel about the way you worship God? How can this vision of God enhance your worship life?

Next Week

Today we entered into the presence of God and found that his power and majesty are too great to be understood; yet he makes himself completely available to sinful men and women. In the coming week, spend time in worshipful prayer, praising God for his power and thanking him for the work of Jesus Christ. Next week we will watch as Jesus, the Lamb of God, opens a mysterious scroll.

Notes on Revelation 4:1–11

SUMMARY: The first vision (1:9–3:22) was of the exalted Christ caring for the first-century church ("what is now," 1:19). In the second vision (4:1–16:21) "what will take place" (1:19; 4:1) in the future is revealed; i.e. the coming of God's kingdom. The second vision has a number of parts to it, of which the first two parts (ch. 4; 5) take place in the throne room of heaven and serve as an introduction to the rest of the vision. The vision begins in heaven with God, who rules the universe. It is important to remember in the midst of the dark days of the end times that the presence of almighty God in heaven is the ultimate reality within which these coming events are being played out.

4:1 *After this I looked.* This is a phrase that usually begins a new division of the narrative. *an open door.* Unlike the door into the kingdom (3:8) and the door into the heart (3:20), this is a door into heaven through which John is invited to pass ("Come up here") and so encounter the next part of his vision.

4:2 *I was in the Spirit.* John is caught up in an ecstatic vision. Such visions are not uncommon in Scripture (1 Kin. 22:19). **One was seated on the throne.** John is granted a vision of God on his throne. John does not so much describe the person or throne; instead he conveys a set of images that seek to capture in words what is surely beyond words. The image of the throne pervades Revelation, occurring more than 40 times.

4:3 What John saw was akin to the luminous sparkling of precious stones and gems. Light was a common image by which God was described (Ps. 104:2; 1 Tim. 6:16). *jasper.* What is called jasper today is opaque, while this heavenly gem is described in 21:11 as a transparent crystal. *carnelian.* A fiery red mineral found in Sardis. *rainbow.* There is an arc of a rainbow around the throne the color of emerald green (unlike a normal rainbow which contains the full spectrum of colors). It is probably better to see these as symbols which seek to convey God arrayed in "unapproachable light, whom no one has seen or can see" (1 Tim. 6:16).

4:4 *24 elders.* There are various interpretations of these figures. Some say they represent the 24 orders of the church of the Old and New Testament (with the 12 patriarchs and the 12 apostles).

Others hold that they are angels who assist in the ruling of the universe. In any case, they function to worship and serve God.

4:5 In the Old Testament, the presence of God was frequently accompanied by thunder and lightning (Ex. 19:16–17; Job 37:2–5; Ps.18:13–15; Ezek.1:13), phenomena that give a sense of his awesome power. *seven fiery torches.* Probably a symbol of the presence of the Holy Spirit.

4:6 *a sea of glass.* For Old Testament parallels to this image see Exodus 24:10 and Ezekiel 1:22. *four living creatures.* These are similar to the creatures ("seraphim," "cherubim") seen in the visions of Isaiah (Isa. 6:1–3) and Ezekiel (Ezek.10:14). They are some sort of angelic order that serves God.

4:7 Their forms suggest different aspects of nature: wild beasts, domesticated animals, human beings and flying creatures. This in turn suggests that they may function to express God's will in all of creation.

4:8 *wings.* This suggests that they are capable of rapid movement. *eyes.* This suggests that they are constantly watching what is happening. They are alert and knowledgeable. *Almighty.* The church, which is about to enter a time of persecution, needs to be reminded that God is a God of all power who will see them through their troubles.

4:9–11 The living creatures and the 24 elders join in praise to God. The living creatures in their song praised God for his essential nature (v. 8), while the elders in their song praise him for his created works.

SESSION 6

The Scroll and the Lamb
SCRIPTURE REVELATION 5:1–14

Last Week

In our previous session, we came before the throne of God, marveling at his incomprehensible character, yet finding joy in the fact that he makes himself freely available to us. This week we will watch as a mysterious scroll is presented in heaven that no creature anywhere from any time in history is able to open. Then we will learn of the One who is worthy to open it.

Ice-Breaker   15 Min.

CONNECT WITH YOUR GROUP

LEADER

Choose one or two of the Ice-Breaker questions. If you have a new group member you may want to do all three. Remember to stick closely to the three-part agenda and the time allowed for each segment.

Music is an important part of life, but what is music to one set of ears may be an unpleasant noise to others. In our Scripture passage for today, we will see how important music is in heaven. Take turns sharing some of your thoughts and experiences with music.

1. What was the best choir or musical group you have ever heard (or participated in)? What was memorable about the group?

2. What is your favorite type of Christian music?

   ○ Traditional hymns.
   ○ Praise songs.
   ○ Contemporary Christian music.
   ○ Southern gospel.
   ○ Other _____.

3. Growing up, what musical instrument did you play? What instrument would you like to play now?

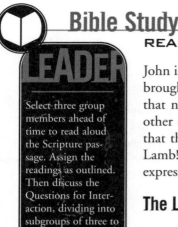

LEADER

Select three group members ahead of time to read aloud the Scripture passage. Assign the readings as outlined. Then discuss the Questions for Interaction, dividing into subgroups of three to six.

John is standing near the throne of God when a mysterious scroll is brought out, sealed with seven seals. He despairs when he learns that nobody who has ever lived, whether human or angel or any other creature, is worthy to open the seals. But suddenly he finds that there is One who *is* worthy—the One who is both Lion and Lamb! Read Revelation 5:1–14, and note the joy and thankfulness expressed in the songs of praise.

The Lamb and the Scroll

Reader One: 5 Then I saw in the right hand of the One seated on the throne a scroll with writing on the inside and on the back, sealed with seven seals. ²I also saw a mighty angel proclaiming in a loud voice,

Reader Two: "Who is worthy to open the scroll and break its seals?"

Reader One: ³But no one in heaven or on earth or under the earth was able to open the scroll or even to look in it. ⁴And I cried and cried because no one was found worthy to open the scroll or even to look in it. ⁵Then one of the elders said to me,

Reader Three: "Stop crying. Look! The Lion from the tribe of Judah, the Root of David, has been victorious so that He may open the scroll and its seven seals."

Reader One: ⁶Then I saw one like a slaughtered lamb standing between the throne and the four living creatures and among the elders. He had seven horns and seven eyes, which are the seven spirits of God sent into all the earth. ⁷He came and took the scroll out of the right hand of the One seated on the throne. ⁸When He took the scroll, the four living creatures and the 24 elders fell down before the Lamb. Each one had a harp and gold bowls filled with incense, which are the prayers of the saints.
    ⁹And they sang a new song:

Reader Two: You are worthy to take the scroll
        and to open its seals;
        because You were slaughtered,
        and You redeemed people for God by Your blood
        from every tribe and language and people and nation.
    ¹⁰You made them a kingdom and priests to our God,
        and they will reign on the earth.

Reader One: ¹¹Then I looked, and heard the voice of many angels around the throne, and also of the living creatures, and of the elders. Their number was countless thousands, plus thousands of thousands. ¹²They said with a loud voice:

Reader Three: The Lamb who was slaughtered is worthy
to receive power and riches
and wisdom and strength
and honor and glory and blessing!

Reader One: ¹³I heard every creature in heaven, on earth, under the earth, on the sea, and everything in them say:

Reader Two: Blessing and honor and glory and dominion
to the One seated on the throne,
and to the Lamb, forever and ever!

Reader Three: ¹⁴The four living creatures said, "Amen," and the elders fell down and worshiped.

Revelation 5:1–14

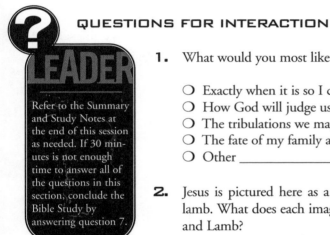

QUESTIONS FOR INTERACTION

Refer to the Summary and Study Notes at the end of this session as needed. If 30 minutes is not enough time to answer all of the questions in this section, conclude the Bible Study by answering question 7.

1. What would you most like to know about the end times?

○ Exactly when it is so I can be ready.
○ How God will judge us.
○ The tribulations we may have to go through.
○ The fate of my family and friends.
○ Other _____.

2. Jesus is pictured here as a victorious lion and as a slaughtered lamb. What does each image suggest? How can he be both Lion and Lamb?

3. Why are the "prayers of the saints" like fragrant incense (v. 8)?

4. Why is Jesus the only one who is worthy to open the scroll?

5. Analyze the three songs of praise in verses 9–13. What do they tell us about the Lamb? Who sings the songs?

6. What would this vision have meant to the persecuted Christians in Asia? What does it mean to you?

7. What do these visions say to us today as we view our out-of-control world? How does that change your perspective on life this week?

GOING DEEPER:

If your group has time and/or wants a challenge, go on to this question.

8. Note that Jesus, as the Lamb, stands between the throne and the "four living creatures" and elders (v. 6). What is the significance of this position? Why does the Lamb stand there and not the Lion?

Caring Time   15 Min.

APPLY THE LESSON AND PRAY FOR ONE ANOTHER

LEADER

Be sure to save at least 15 minutes for this important time of prayer and encouragement. Continue to encourage group members to invite new people to the group. Remind them that this group is for learning and sharing, but also for reaching out to others.

Jesus Christ, as both God and man, gave his own life like a sacrificial Lamb so that all people of every nation, tribe and tongue might come to have free access to the presence of God. It is this that gives him—and only him—the right to open this mysterious scroll. It also urges us, as his followers, to sing his praises. Encourage and support one another now with a time of sharing, praise and prayer.

1. Lately, what kind of fragrance do your prayers make to God?

   ○ Roses.
   ○ Honeysuckle.
   ○ Red cedar.
   ○ Stinky weeds.
   ○ Other _____.

2. What aspect of Christ's character would you most like to praise this week?

3. What is something you feel God may be calling you to do?

Next Week

This week we listened as every living creature in all of creation sang the praises of Jesus Christ, the Lamb who was slaughtered. In the coming week, spend some time reflecting on the character, power and work of Jesus, singing his praises in prayer or song. Next week we will watch as the Lamb begins to open the seals on this mysterious scroll.

Notes on Revelation 5:1–14

SUMMARY: The scene moves from its focus on God and his surrounding attendants to the Lamb, who opens the sacred scroll and so initiates the final conflict with Satan and his forces.

5:1 *the right hand of the One seated on the throne.* It is God who holds the whole of human history in his hand. He is sovereign, and no matter how strong evil may appear to be it is he who controls the ultimate flow of events. *a scroll.* The nature of this scroll is not clear. The best guess is that this scroll is like the one given to Ezekiel, containing "words of lament and mourning and woe" (Ezek. 2:10, NIV). The nature of this prophecy is then described in chapters 7–22. *seven.* The number seven occurs frequently in Revelation, as indeed it does in the rest of the Bible. It has to do with completeness; it relates to the fullness of something. God created the earth in six days and rested on the seventh. As the world began in seven days, so it will end by a series of sevens. *seals.* The scroll is rolled up and sealed along its edge with seven wax seals that ensure the secrecy of its contents. The seals must be broken in order for the contents to be read. As each seal is broken, a momentous event takes place.

5:2–3 The call goes out across creation ("in heaven or on earth or under the earth") for someone to bring history to its conclusion, but no one is found.

5:4 So overwhelming is the thought that God's final action in history has to be postponed for want of a worthy mediator that John bursts into tears.

5:5 The elder calms John. There is one who is worthy to perform this task. It is Christ who can and will reveal where history is going and how it will end. The meaning of history (which is contained in the scroll) cannot be known apart from Christ. *The Lion from the tribe of Judah.* An ancient title for the Messiah (Gen. 49:9–10), which was in use in the first century. The image is of a conquering King. *the Root of David.* Another messianic title, referring this time to the fact that the Messiah will

come from the royal family of David (Isa. 11:1). *victorious.* By his death on the cross, Jesus won a great victory over evil, sin and death (Col. 2:15; 2 Tim. 1:10; Heb. 2:14–15). Though this victory is real and eternal, its full realization will occur only at the end of time. This assertion functions to confirm once more that despite the great battles that lie ahead, the outcome is certain.

5:6 *a slaughtered lamb.* The Lion has become a Lamb. The final victory of the conquering Messiah is only possible because of the death of the Lamb of God. In the Old Testament a lamb was sacrificed each Passover, reminding the nation that God had spared them and delivered them from the bondage of Egypt (Ex. 12:13). Interestingly, the connection was not made between the slain lamb and the Messiah prior to New Testament revelation, despite the prophecy in Isaiah 53. Until Jesus, people could not conceive of a conquering Messiah who was slain as a sacrificial lamb. *seven horns.* A horn is a symbol of power in the Old Testament (Deut. 33:17; Ps. 18:2). Seven horns would represent the fullness of power (Matt. 28:18). *seven eyes.* He also has fullness of vision and omniscience (Zech. 4:10). *the seven spirits.* The work of Christ on earth is done by the Holy Spirit that is, once again, pictured by means of this symbol (4:5).

5:8 When the Lamb grasps the scroll of history, the whole of heaven bursts into a song of praise. *harp.* The instrument of praise in the Psalms (Ps. 33:2). *incense.* Incense was used in Old Testament worship (Deut. 33:10). Here it stands for the prayers of God's people.

5:9 *a new song.* A special song composed for this momentous occasion when a whole new order of reality is about to be instituted. *redeemed.* Ransomed—a word used to describe the freeing of a slave from bondage by the payment of a price. The purchase price, in this case, was the blood of Christ. What it bought was the freedom of men and women from the bondage of sin. *from every tribe and language and people and nation.* Christ redeems people from the whole of mankind—past, present and future—by this great and terrible payment.

5:10 *a kingdom and priests.* The result is that they have become God's people and God's priests. They will share in God's rule and they will have access to his presence. *reign on the earth.* In order for his people to reign on earth, his kingdom must be established there in fullness. Thus it is necessary to break the seals and so bring about the kingdom.

5:11 Myriads of angels join this heavenly chorus.

5:13 The rest of creation joins in the singing.

SESSION 7
Opening the Seals
SCRIPTURE REVELATION 6:1–17

Last Week

The majesty and power of Jesus Christ was our focus in last week's session. We saw Jesus as both the Lion and the Lamb, and listened as the heavenly host praised him for his sacrificial death that bought humanity's redemption. We were also comforted by the fact that God is sovereign and has everything under control. This week we will watch as Jesus begins to undo the seals on the scroll, and will tremble as we see the terrible things that follow.

Ice-Breaker   15 Min.
CONNECT WITH YOUR GROUP

LEADER

Open with a word of prayer, and then introduce and welcome new group members. If there are no new members, choose one or two of the Ice-Breaker questions to get started. If there are new members, then discuss all three.

Life is full of sounds, colors and experiences. All of our varied experiences—both good and bad—help to make us who we are. From our personal preferences to the rough things we've gone through, each of us has some interesting story to tell. Take turns sharing your thoughts about the following questions.

1. If you were an ancient soldier, which weapon would you like to carry and why?

   ○ Sword.
   ○ Bow.
   ○ Club.
   ○ Lance.
   ○ I would have been the medic.
   ○ I would have been protesting violent acts.
   ○ Other _____.

2. What is your favorite color?

3. Have you ever been in an earthquake? What was it like?

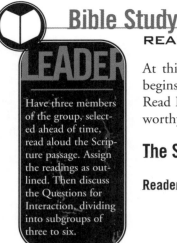

READ SCRIPTURE AND DISCUSS

At this point in John's vision, the Lamb takes up the scroll and begins to open its seals. This begins a very terrifying series of events. Read Revelation 6:1–17, and note why no one but God himself is worthy to loose the seals.

The Six Seals

Leader

Have three members of the group, selected ahead of time, read aloud the Scripture passage. Assign the readings as outlined. Then discuss the Questions for Interaction, dividing into subgroups of three to six.

Reader One: 6 Then I saw the Lamb open one of the seven seals, and I heard one of the four living creatures say with a voice like thunder, "Come!" ²I looked, and there was a white horse. The horseman on it had a bow; a crown was given to him, and he went out as a victor to conquer.

Reader Two: ³When He opened the second seal, I heard the second living creature say, "Come!" ⁴Then another horse went out, a fiery red one, and its horseman was empowered to take peace from the earth, so that people would slaughter one another. And a large sword was given to him.

Reader Three: ⁵When He opened the third seal, I heard the third living creature say, "Come!" And I looked, and there was a black horse. The horseman on it had a balance scale in his hand. ⁶Then I heard something like a voice among the four living creatures say,

Reader Two: "A quart of wheat for a denarius, and three quarts of barley for a denarius—but do not harm the olive oil and the wine."

Reader Three: ⁷When He opened the fourth seal, I heard the voice of the fourth living creature say, "Come!" ⁸And I looked, and there was a pale green horse. The horseman on it was named Death, and Hades was following after him. Authority was given to them over a fourth of the earth, to kill by the sword, by famine, by plague, and by the wild animals of the earth. ⁹When He opened the fifth seal, I saw under the altar the souls of those slaughtered because of God's word and the testimony they had. ¹⁰They cried out with a loud voice:

Reader One: "O Lord, holy and true, how long until You judge and avenge our blood from those who live on the earth?"

Reader Two: ¹¹So a white robe was given to each of them, and they were told to rest a little while longer until the number of their fellow slaves and their brothers, who were going to be killed just as they had been, would be completed. ¹²Then I saw Him open the sixth seal. A violent earthquake occurred; the sun turned black like sackcloth made of goat hair; the entire moon became like blood; ¹³the stars of heaven fell to the earth as a fig tree drops its unripe figs when shaken by a high wind; ¹⁴the sky separated like a scroll being rolled up; and every mountain and island was moved from its place.

Reader Three: ¹⁵Then the kings of the earth, the nobles, the military commanders, the rich, the powerful, and every slave and free person hid in the caves and among the rocks of the mountains. ¹⁶And they said to the mountains and to the rocks,

Reader One: "Fall on us and hide us from the face of the One seated on the throne and from the wrath of the Lamb, ¹⁷because the great day of Their wrath has come! And who is able to stand?"

Revelation 6:1–17

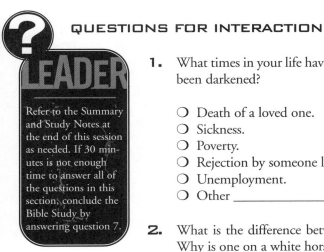

QUESTIONS FOR INTERACTION

Refer to the Summary and Study Notes at the end of this session as needed. If 30 minutes is not enough time to answer all of the questions in this section, conclude the Bible Study by answering question 7.

1. What times in your life have made you feel as though the sun had been darkened?

○ Death of a loved one.
○ Sickness.
○ Poverty.
○ Rejection by someone loved.
○ Unemployment.
○ Other _____.

2. What is the difference between the first and second horseman? Why is one on a white horse (v. 2) and the other on a "fiery red" horse (v. 4)?

3. Each of the four horsemen is given power, authority or instructions. Who is giving these things? What does this teach us about the power of calamity, evil and death?

4. Why are the souls of the martyrs found under the altar?

5. The martyrs cry out to God, "How long?" His answer is, "a little while longer" (v. 11). How can God's concept of "a little while" sometimes seem different from our perspective? In eternity, whose perspective will prove true?

6. God tells the martyrs that the number of those to be killed for the Gospel must be completed. What does this show concerning God's control over the affairs of humanity?

7. When have you felt that God's sense of "a little while" was not such a little while? In retrospect, was it truly a little while or a long while?

GOING DEEPER:

If your group has time and/or wants a challenge, go on to this question.

8. Do you think that these calamities refer to the end times, to the sufferings in the world throughout history, or both? Why?

Caring Time   15 Min.

APPLY THE LESSON AND PRAY FOR ONE ANOTHER

LEADER

Continue to encourage group members to invite new people to the group. Close the group prayer by thanking God for each member and for this time together.

No time of suffering or discipline seems short while we are in the midst of it, but God makes it clear to us through John's vision that the eternal perspective is quite different from our own. In the meantime, however, we must support one another during times of trial or sorrow.

1. Have you been undergoing some form of sorrow "for a little while"? How can the group help?

2. How has this group been an encouragement to you?

3. What can you do in the coming week for someone who is hurting?

Next Week

Today we watched breathlessly as the Lamb began to open the seals on the scroll. They revealed some terrifying things, but through it all John keeps reminding us that God is in total control. In the coming week, pray for those who are suffering for "a little while." If you are suffering yourself, ask God to strengthen you to endure faithfully. Next week we will see multitudes of God's redeemed singing his praises!

SUMMARY: The vision in the throne room of heaven (ch. 4–5) sets the stage for the unfolding judgment of the second vision (ch. 6–16), beginning here with the opening of the seven seals (6:1–8:1). The seven seals must be broken before the contents of the scroll can be read. What is contained here is a symbolic representation of the realities people in all times and places experience throughout history as they await the final judgment of God.

6:1–2 The first seal is broken by the Lamb himself, the only one worthy to set in motion these momentous events.

6:1 *Come!* One of the living creatures summons the first of the four apocalyptic horsemen. The images that follow are similar to those in Zechariah's visions (Zech. 1:8–17; 6:1–8).

6:2 *a white horse.* There has been much debate about the identity of the rider on the white horse. One suggestion is that he symbolizes military conquest, an image in line with the identity of the other three riders. Another suggestion is that the rider on the white horse symbolizes the preaching of the Gospel throughout the world prior to the end. The bow is used in the Old Testament as a symbol of divine victories (Hab. 3:9). In Revelation, white is generally a symbol of Christ (1:14; 14:14; 19:11,14). Furthermore, unlike the coming of the other three horsemen, no calamities follow after this rider.

6:3–4 The second seal is broken and a red horse and rider appear. There is no ambiguity about this figure—it is a symbol of bloodshed and war.

6:5 The third seal is broken and a black horse and rider are called forth, symbolizing a time of great scarcity verging on famine. *balance scale.* A balance used for measuring out grain.

6:6 Food is sold at inflated prices—over 10 times what it should cost. *a denarius.* In those days, a man earned a denarius (a Roman coin) for a day's work (Matt. 20:2). This was normally enough to feed a whole family, but now it could only buy enough wheat—the staple food of the area—for a single person. Three times as much barley could be purchased, but barley is less nutritious. *do not harm the olive oil and the wine.* A limitation is placed upon the rider of the black horse. Grain is easily destroyed by drought, but the drought is not to be so severe as to damage the deeper roots of the olive trees or grape vines.

6:7–8 The fourth horse and rider represent death from various causes. These are the "four dreadful judgments" in Ezekiel 14:21.

6:8 *a pale green horse.* The color of a corpse. *Hades.* It is not clear whether Hades is following behind Death on foot, on another horse, or on the same horse. Still, the image is clear. After death comes the grave or the underworld. Hades was understood to be the place where the dead resided as they awaited the final judgment. *a fourth of the earth.* There is a limitation placed upon Death. It threatens all of life, but is not permitted to totally do away with all of it. *kill by the sword.* This is death by murder, war or violence. *famine.* The issue is no longer scarcity (as with the black horse), but a severe lack of food that leads to death.

6:9 A new scene unfolds with the breaking of the fifth seal. Those who have been martyred in the name of God are pictured under the altar. *God's word.* This is the message of the Gospel. They were slain because of their confession of Jesus as Lord. *the testimony they had.* This probably refers not to testimony as "witnessing" to others about their faith, but rather to the fact that they had maintained even unto death their faithfulness to the witness Jesus had given. They remained loyal to the Gospel.

6:10 *holy.* The martyrs appeal to his holiness. He is beyond all evil and so can be relied upon to right the wrong done to them. *those who live on the earth.* In Revelation, this phrase refers to those who are hostile to God.

6:12–13 *earthquake.* The very trembling of the earth is often associated with the presence of God (Ex. 19:18; Isa. 2:19; Hag. 2:6). *sun/moon/stars.* Even the predictable, well-ordered movement of the heavenly bodies goes awry (Isa. 34:4; Acts 2:20).

6:14 *separated like a scroll.* The image is of a papyrus scroll stretched out across the sky, which snaps in the middle and rolls up quickly on either side.

6:15 *kings/nobles/military commanders/the rich/the powerful.* Even those in power who would have been secure in most circumstances are undone by these events.

6:16 *the wrath of the Lamb.* An unusual phrase, since a lamb is thought of as gentle.

6:17 *the great day of Their wrath.* There are many titles used to describe this period of time. In this case the focus is on judgment; on the fact that those who have rebelled against God will face his judgment.

Visions of Multitudes

SCRIPTURE REVELATION 7:1–17

Last Week

In our previous session, we watched in terror as the Lamb began to undo the seals on the scroll. We were reminded once again that God is in control, even in the midst of these terrible events. This week we will turn our eyes to those who are standing around us, and we will discover vast multitudes of people and angels—every race, nation and tongue—singing the praises of the Almighty.

Ice-Breaker   15 Min.

CONNECT WITH YOUR GROUP

LEADER

Open with a word of prayer, and be sure to welcome and introduce new group members. Choose one, two or all three of the Ice-Breaker questions.

All of us are members of the same family—the human race—yet we are each unique individuals. Take turns sharing how you express your own individuality.

1. What colors do you tend to wear most?

- ○ White.
- ○ Black.
- ○ Bright colors.
- ○ Pastels.
- ○ Plaid.
- ○ Other _____.

2. What do you like to do on a windy day?

- ○ Sail.
- ○ Fly a kite.
- ○ Stay indoors.
- ○ Other _____.

3. How do you react to large crowds? What event have you attended that attracted the largest number of people?

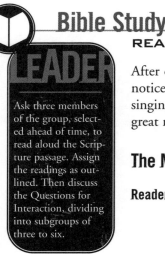

READ SCRIPTURE AND DISCUSS

After opening the first six seals of the scroll, we take a moment to notice the throngs who are gathered around the throne of God, singing his praises. Read Revelation 7:1–17, and rejoice with the great multitudes in white robes.

The Multitudes

Reader One: 7 After this I saw four angels standing at the four corners of the earth, restraining the four winds of the earth so that no wind could blow on the earth or on the sea or on any tree. [2]Then I saw another angel rise up from the east, who had the seal of the living God. He cried out in a loud voice to the four angels who were empowered to harm the earth and the sea:

Reader Two: [3]"Don't harm the earth or the sea or the trees until we seal the slaves of our God on their foreheads."

Reader One: [4]And I heard the number of those who were sealed:

Reader Three: 144,000 sealed from every tribe of the sons of Israel:
[5]12,000 sealed from the tribe of Judah,
12,000 from the tribe of Reuben,
12,000 from the tribe of Gad,
[6]12,000 from the tribe of Asher,
12,000 from the tribe of Naphtali,
12,000 from the tribe of Manasseh,
[7]12,000 from the tribe of Simeon,
12,000 from the tribe of Levi,
12,000 from the tribe of Issachar,
[8]12,000 from the tribe of Zebulun,
12,000 from the tribe of Joseph,
12,000 sealed from the tribe of Benjamin.

Reader One: [9]After this I looked, and there was a vast multitude from every nation, tribe, people, and language, which no one could number, standing before the throne and before the Lamb. They were robed in white with palm branches in their hands. [10]And they cried out in a loud voice:

Reader Two: Salvation belongs to our God who is seated on the throne and to the Lamb!

Reader One: [11]All the angels stood around the throne, the elders, and the four living creatures, and they fell on their faces before the throne and worshiped God, [12]saying:

Reader Three: Amen! Blessing and glory and wisdom
and thanksgiving and honor
and power and strength,
be to our God forever and ever. Amen.

Reader One: ¹³Then one of the elders asked me,

Reader Two: "Who are these people robed in white, and where did they come from?"

Reader One: ¹⁴I said to him, "Sir, you know."
Then he told me:

Reader Three: These are the ones coming out of the great tribulation.
They washed their robes and made them white
in the blood of the Lamb.
¹⁵For this reason they are before the throne of God,
and they serve Him day and night in His sanctuary.
The One seated on the throne will shelter them:
¹⁶no longer will they hunger; no longer will they thirst;
no longer will the sun strike them, or any heat.
¹⁷Because the Lamb who is at the center of the throne will shepherd them;
He will guide them to springs of living waters,
and God will wipe away every tear from their eyes.

Revelation 7:1–17

QUESTIONS FOR INTERACTION

Refer to the Summary and Study Notes at the end of this session as needed. If 30 minutes is not enough time to answer all of the questions in this section, conclude the Bible Study by answering question 7.

1. God has paused in the opening of the seals; following this part of the vision will come more woe. Why does God choose to take this "interlude" here?

○ He wants us to understand that he will protect us during this difficult time.
○ He knows that worship and praise will strengthen us as we face tribulations.
○ He wants us to be encouraged by seeing the large numbers of fellow believers.
○ Other _____.

2. How is God's complete control demonstrated again in this passage?

3. Jesus is the only one who could break the seals on the scroll. What does this imply about the seals on the foreheads of the "slaves" (v. 3)?

4. Who are the people who gather at the throne to sing God's praises? Is anyone excluded or exempt from worshiping God?

5. What do the white robes signify? The palm branches?

6. God promises to "wipe away every tear" from the eyes of his "slaves" (v. 17). When will this happen? If they have tears to be wiped away, what does this suggest about the lives of God's people?

7. What sort of seal has God placed on your life? How is this seal evident to other Christians? To non-Christians?

GOING DEEPER:

If your group has time and/or wants a challenge, go on to this question.

8. Why are the 144,000 sealed on their foreheads? Why not their hearts or hands?

Caring Time   15 Min.

APPLY THE LESSON AND PRAY FOR ONE ANOTHER

LEADER

Have you started talking with your group about their mission—perhaps by sharing the vision of multiplying into two groups by the end of this study of Revelation?

One day every human who has ever lived will stand before God—some to be given robes of white, others to be cast out of God's presence. Today we have met the innumerable multitudes who will be dressed in white. Gather around each other now for a time of sharing and prayer, remembering those who are weeping, whether outwardly or inwardly.

1. Whom do you know who needs Jesus to guide him or her to the "springs of living waters" (v. 17)? How can the group pray for this person?

2. Will you one day be among those dressed in white, praising God for your salvation? If you're not sure, how can the group help?

3. Are there tears in your eyes this week? How would you ask God to wipe them away?

Next Week

Today we watched as an innumerable multitude of God's people bowed in worship at his throne. In the coming week, bow your own knees in worship, thanking God for his salvation and praising him for his power. If you are not certain that you will one day join this eternal throng, ask God to grant you his gift of eternal life through the blood of the Lamb, Jesus Christ. Next week we will watch as the Lamb opens the seventh seal.

SUMMARY: Chapter 7 is a dramatic interlude between the opening of the sixth and the seventh seals, in which the security of the faithful is set in contrast to the panic of the world. The earth is pictured as a great square, with an angel at each corner holding back a lethal wind until the 144,000 can be sealed. The focus then shifts from before the Tribulation to after it. A multitude stands before God, consisting of people from across the planet. John's view has moved beyond the dark time of the Tribulation to the final victory, which will be the ultimate reality.

7:3 *seal.* Probably similar to the signet ring that kings used to authenticate documents by its imprint. The purpose of this seal is to mark out God's people so that they will be spared from the plagues that are to come (9:4). This is similar to the time of the Exodus, when the tenth plague brought death to the firstborn of those households not marked by blood over the door.

7:5 Judah heads the list, not Reuben, who belongs in that place as Jacob's oldest son (Gen. 49:3). Probably the reason for this is that Christ came from the tribe of Judah (5:5). *12,000.* This number (and the total number of 144,000—12 squared, multiplied by one thousand) may be symbolic, conveying the idea of completeness: 12,000 are sealed from each of the 12 tribes. The full complement is sealed. It may also be literal, the actual number of those faithful during the Tribulation.

7:10 The song they sing is not, as one might expect, one of gratitude to God for their deliverance. Rather, it is a song of praise to God for his work of salvation. Their salvation involves more than just deliverance from the Tribulation.

7:11–12 The heavenly beings—the angels, elders and four living creatures—chime in with their own song: a sevenfold doxology of praise in which they heap up, one upon another, God's attributes.

7:12 *glory.* A reference to the brightness of God, his divine luminous presence. *thanksgiving.* For his great work of salvation by which he has overcome evil and established his kingdom. *honor.* The greatness of his work is acknowledged publicly. *power.* When God acts, he cannot be overcome.

strength. His redemptive work in the events of history.

7:14 *the ones coming out of.* These are the martyrs from the Great Tribulation: those who maintained their faith to the point of death. *the great tribulation.* This event is mentioned in both the Old and New Testament. Daniel 12:1 refers to the "time of distress" (literally, "tribulation" in Greek) that will come. Jesus picks up these words of Daniel and expands upon them: "For at that time there will be great tribulation, the kind that hasn't taken place since the beginning of the world until now, and never will again! Unless those days were not cut short, no one would survive. But because of the elect those days will be cut short" (Matt. 24:21–22). Though suffering has been the lot of God's people down through the ages (John 16:33; 2 Tim. 3:12), this will be a time of unparalleled persecution and conflict.

7:15 *will shelter them.* A reference to the tabernacle in the wilderness (Lev. 26:11–13) where God's presence dwelt. That his tent is over them would mean that they are now drawn into his presence, rather than standing outside the tent (Ezek. 37:27; Zech. 2:10).

7:16 *no longer will they hunger/thirst.* Such a promise was especially significant to people of that era who knew famine and where, in many regions, water was scarce. This promise, however, goes beyond physical provision. The satisfying of hunger and thirst is used in Scripture as a metaphor for spiritual satisfaction (Matt. 5:6; John 6:35). *sun/heat.* Again, to people living in the Middle East, the promise of shelter from the intensity of the sun was welcome indeed. This also has spiritual implications.

7:17 *the Lamb ... will shepherd them.* A curious image—the Lamb becomes the shepherd (who tends the flock of lambs). However, with the fluid language of visions, it is appropriate that both these descriptions of the Messiah be expressed. In the Old Testament, God is frequently portrayed as the shepherd of his people; i.e., the one who gives guidance, provides for needs and protects his flock (Ps. 23:1; Isa. 40:11; Ezek. 34:23). In the New Testament, Jesus is pictured as the Good Shepherd, (John 10:1–30; 21:15–17). *He will guide them to springs of living waters.* His main role here is to lead the flock to the water of life, which is the presence of God (John 4:14). *wipe away every tear.* Their suffering is now past. There is a new reality in which tears are not necessary. Joy will be their portion (21:4).

SESSION 9
The Trumpets, Part 1
SCRIPTURE REVELATION 8:1–13

Last Week

In our previous session, we listened as thousands upon thousands bowed at the throne of God and sang his praises. We rejoiced in the fact that God has put his seal upon us and will guide us to "living waters." He will also wipe every tear from our eyes. This week the joyous roar of praises will die into a sudden silence, as the Lamb opens the seventh seal on the scroll.

Ice-Breaker   15 Min.
CONNECT WITH YOUR GROUP

LEADER

Open with a word of prayer. Welcome and introduce any new group members. Choose one, two or all three Ice-Breaker questions, depending on your group's needs.

Crowds can be fun and exhilarating, but sometimes we just need some peace and quiet. Even Jesus needed time by himself for prayer and reflection. Take turns sharing your experiences with moments of solitude.

1. When do you enjoy solitude and silence?

   ○ When working.
   ○ At church.
   ○ In the evening.
   ○ In the morning.
   ○ Never.
   ○ Always.
   ○ Other _____.

2. As a child, were you shy and quiet or outgoing and loud? How about now?

3. What kind of music helps you to relax?

READ SCRIPTURE AND DISCUSS

It is time now for the Lamb to loose the seventh seal on the scroll, which unleashes a terrible series of calamity and woe. This seal will be broken down into several smaller parts, including the four trumpets that will sound forth in this section. Read Revelation 8:1–13, and note the importance of prayer before the trumpets are blown.

The Seventh Seal

Reader One: 8 When He opened the seventh seal, there was silence in heaven for about half an hour. ²Then I saw the seven angels who stand in the presence of God; seven trumpets were given to them. ³Another angel, with a gold incense burner, came and stood at the altar. He was given a large amount of incense to offer with the prayers of all the saints on the gold altar in front of the throne. ⁴The smoke of the incense, with the prayers of the saints, went up in the presence of God from the angel's hand. ⁵The angel took the incense burner, filled it with fire from the altar, and hurled it to the earth; there were thunders, rumblings, lightnings, and an earthquake. ⁶And the seven angels who had the seven trumpets prepared to blow them.

Reader Two: ⁷The first angel blew his trumpet, and hail and fire, mixed with blood, were hurled to the earth. So a third of the earth was burned up, a third of the trees were burned up, and all the green grass was burned up. ⁸The second angel blew his trumpet, and something like a great mountain ablaze with fire was hurled into the sea. So a third of the sea became blood, ⁹a third of the living creatures in the sea died, and a third of the ships were destroyed.

Reader Three: ¹⁰The third angel blew his trumpet, and a great star, blazing like a torch, fell from heaven. It fell on a third of the rivers and springs of water. ¹¹The name of the star is Wormwood, and a third of the waters became wormwood. So, many of the people died from the waters, because they had been made bitter.

Reader Four: ¹²The fourth angel blew his trumpet, and a third of the sun was struck, a third of the moon, and a third of the stars, so that a third of them were darkened. A third of the day was without light, and the night as well. ¹³I looked, and I heard an eagle, flying in mid-heaven, saying in a loud voice, "Woe! Woe! Woe to those who live on the earth, because of the remaining trumpet blasts that the three angels are about to sound!"

Revelation 8:1–13

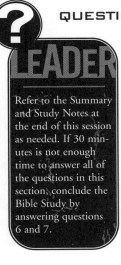

QUESTIONS FOR INTERACTION

LEADER

Refer to the Summary and Study Notes at the end of this session as needed. If 30 minutes is not enough time to answer all of the questions in this section, conclude the Bible Study by answering questions 6 and 7.

1. What affect does profound silence have on you?

　○ Loneliness.
　○ Thoughtfulness.
　○ Worship.
　○ Peace.
　○ Fear.
　○ Other _____.

2. Why is there silence in heaven after opening the seventh seal? Why half an hour?

3. Note that the altar is right in front of the throne. Why is this important? What does this tell us about our prayers?

4. The same fire that burns the incense on the altar is hurled to the earth in judgment. What does this suggest?

5. If these are figurative pictures of calamities, what might each represent? Why is "a third" repeated so frequently?

6. Have you ever spent a long period in silent contemplation and prayer? What did you glean from the experience?

7. Wormwood is bitterness. Has bitterness ever affected your life, directly or indirectly? How have you dealt with this?

GOING DEEPER:

If your group has time and/or wants a challenge, go on to this question.

8. Isaiah predicted that the Messiah would be born from a virgin (Isa. 7:14), an impossibility that was literally fulfilled. In the same way, it is possible that some or all of these calamities might literally come true. How might any of these trumpets come to pass literally?

Caring Time

APPLY THE LESSON AND PRAY FOR ONE ANOTHER

LEADER

Have you identified someone in the group that could be a leader for a new small group when your group divides? How could you encourage and mentor that person?

Life can deal each of us hard blows, and at times it is easy to let bitterness creep in. The most important issue of all, however, is to be sure that we have been given the gift of eternal life. Share your responses to the following questions before closing in prayer.

1. What do you look forward to most about these meetings?

2. Do you know with confidence that you have been saved from the final "woe," eternal separation from God? How would you like the group to pray for you or someone else who is seeking God.

3. Are you struggling with bitterness toward someone? How will you "root it out" of your life?

Next Week

Today we have witnessed some of the horrors that will come from the judgment of God upon a sinful race, listening to trumpet blasts of woe and warning. In the coming week, examine your own life for things that are not pleasing to God, such as the "root of bitterness" that springs up so easily. If you are not certain that you are among God's redeemed, ask God to forgive your sins through the blood of Jesus Christ. Next week we will hear more trumpet blasts, calling mankind to repent.

SUMMARY: It is debated whether this section about the seven trumpets represents the contents of the seventh seal (v. 1) or whether the seven trumpets are another way of rehearsing the scope of history from the perspective of God's judgments, which he has continually brought upon the earth in an attempt to move people to repent. The former view sees Revelation as a chronologically progressive account of the end, while the latter view sees this book as a series of overlapping visions in which the broad sweep of history is considered from different perspectives, all of which culminate in God's triumph over all evil.

8:1 The breaking of the seventh seal opens the scroll so that the events of the end times can be revealed. *the seventh seal.* Unlike the other seals (with the possible exception of the first seal), the breaking of this seal brings no judgment. There is simply silence. The nature of this silence is not clear. Some say it represents the beginning of eternal rest for the multitudes, but this is out of character with the other seals. Others suggest that it is the time when the prayers of the saints are heard (vv. 3–4). Probably the silence is meant to indicate a moment of suspense before the events of the trumpets unfold.

8:2 *the seven angels.* Who these are is not defined, though they appear to be a specific group of heavenly beings. The Bible does not mention seven angels but other Jewish literature speaks of "the seven holy angels who present the prayers of the saints and enter into the presence of the glory of the Holy One" (Tobit 12:15), and in 1 Enoch 20:2–8 the names of these seven archangels are listed. *trumpets.* In the Old Testament, trumpets are used for various purposes: to signal various activities (Num. 10:1–10); as part of worship and celebration (Num. 10:10; 29:1); in war (Josh. 6); and at coronations (1 Kin. 1:34). Here in Revelation, however, they have the more ominous purpose of announcing and loosing eschatological plagues.

8:3–5 There is a short period of preparation before the sounding of the first trumpet. The seven angels prepare to sound the seven trumpets and the other angel mingles the incense and the prayers of the saints and then flings the censer to earth. The thunder, lightning and earthquakes are all phenomena associated with God's judgment.

8:3 *incense burner.* The fire pan that held the hot coals used to burn incense (Ex. 27:3; 1 Kin. 7:50).

8:7 The second series of calamities begins. As will become evident, the aim of these acts of judgment is to lead people to repentance (9:20; 16:10–11). *fire.* The fire that is mixed with hail may be lightning. *blood.* Probably a reference to the color of the storm, not the destruction it caused. *A third of the earth was burned up.* The first plague destroys a third of the earth's vegetation. The fact that a third of the earth is pictured as being afflicted represents a severe judgment (Ex. 9:13–35).

8:8–9 The second plague is unique; it is impossible to parallel it with any known natural event (e.g., a volcano). It destroys a third of the sea, along with a third of the fish under the sea and a third of the boats on top of the sea. This plague is similar to what happened to the Nile in Exodus 7:20–21.

8:10–11 During the third plague, a great meteor falls from the sky and poisons a third of the fresh water.

8:11 *Wormwood.* A plant that has a bitter taste.

8:12 The fourth plague strikes the heavenly bodies. A third of the sun, moon and stars go dark. This is similar to the ninth plague in Egypt (Ex. 10:21–23). *darkened.* It was not just that the intensity of the light was reduced by a third; there was absolute darkness for a third of the time.

8:13 The first four trumpets have been sounded and four plagues have fallen upon the earth. Prior to the next two plagues (which will fall upon human beings), a warning is sounded. ***Woe!*** The triple "Woe" corresponds to the final three trumpets (9:12). ***those who live on the earth.*** These plagues will come upon those who are hostile to God. Somehow the church—those who have God's seal upon them—will be spared (9:4).

The Trumpets, Part 2

SCRIPTURE REVELATION 9:1-21

Last Week

Our focus in last week's session was on the terrible woes pronounced by the first four trumpets. We were reminded of the importance of prayer as we face difficulties in our life, and how bitterness can only cause death and destruction. This week we will watch as two more trumpet blasts unleash further suffering and woe.

Ice-Breaker   15 Min.

CONNECT WITH YOUR GROUP

LEADER

Choose one or two of the Ice-Breaker questions. If you have a new group member you may want to do all three. Remember to stick closely to the three-part agenda and the time allowed for each segment.

Disaster can strike at any moment, in any form. Sometimes disaster will leave us stunned; other times it just seems like part of life. Take turns sharing about some of your experiences with disaster.

1. What is the most common "disaster" at your house?

○ Spilled milk.
○ Dirty diapers.
○ Stress overload.
○ Overdue bills.
○ Leaking roof.
○ Broken car.
○ Other _____.

2. Have you ever been stung or bitten by one of the following creatures?

○ Bee.
○ Fire ants.
○ Scorpion.
○ Snake.
○ Spider.
○ Dog or cat.
○ Other _____.

3. What natural disaster have you experienced? What happened?

READ SCRIPTURE AND DISCUSS

When the seventh seal was opened, we heard several loud trumpets declaring a variety of woes upon the earth. We now continue for two more trumpets, also declaring some terrible things for mankind. In this section, we will be dealing, once again, with difficult imagery, but the main message of God still comes through loud and clear—repent and be saved. Read Revelation 9:1–21, and note how the people who survive still do not repent of their sins.

More Trumpets

Reader One: 9 The fifth angel blew his trumpet, and I saw a star that had fallen from heaven to earth. The key to the shaft of the abyss was given to him. ²He opened the shaft of the abyss, and smoke came up out of the shaft like smoke from a great furnace so that the sun and the air were darkened by the smoke from the shaft. ³Then out of the smoke locusts came to the earth, and power was given to them like the power that scorpions have on the earth. ⁴They were told not to harm the grass of the earth, or any green plant, or any tree, but only people who do not have God's seal on their foreheads. ⁵They were not permitted to kill them, but were to torment them for five months; their torment is like the torment caused by a scorpion when it strikes a man. ⁶In those days people will seek death and will not find it; they will long to die, but death will flee from them.

Reader Two: ⁷The appearance of the locusts was like horses equipped for battle. On their heads were something like gold crowns; their faces were like men's faces; ⁸they had hair like women's hair; their teeth were like lions' teeth; ⁹they had chests like iron breastplates; the sound of their wings was like the sound of chariots with many horses rushing into battle; ¹⁰and they had tails with stingers, like scorpions, so that with their tails they had the power to harm people for five months. ¹¹They had as their king the angel of the abyss; his name in Hebrew is Abaddon, and in Greek he has the name Apollyon. ¹²The first woe has passed. There are still two more woes to come after this.

Reader Three: ¹³The sixth angel blew his trumpet. From the four horns of the gold altar that is before God, I heard a voice ¹⁴say to the sixth angel who had the trumpet, "Release the four angels bound at the great river Euphrates." ¹⁵So the four angels who were prepared for the hour, day, month, and year were released to kill a third of the human race. ¹⁶The number of mounted troops was 200 million; I heard their number. ¹⁷This is how I saw the horses in my vision: The horsemen had breastplates that were fiery red, hyacinth blue, and sulfur yellow. The heads of the horses were like lions' heads, and from their mouths came fire, smoke, and sulfur. ¹⁸A third of the human race was killed by these three plagues – by the fire, the smoke, and the sulfur that came from their mouths. [19]For the power of the horses is in their mouths and in their tails, because their tails, like snakes, have heads, and they inflict injury with them.

Reader One: [20]The rest of the people, who were not killed by these plagues, did not repent of the works of their hands to stop worshiping demons and idols of gold, silver, bronze, stone, and wood, which are not able to see, hear, or walk. [21]And they did not repent of their murders, their sorceries, their sexual immorality, or their thefts.

Revelation 9:1–21

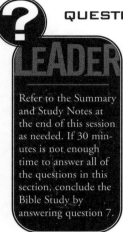

QUESTIONS FOR INTERACTION

Refer to the Summary and Study Notes at the end of this session as needed. If 30 minutes is not enough time to answer all of the questions in this section, conclude the Bible Study by answering question 7.

1. When have you seen, whether at the time or in retrospect, that God was working together all the details and timing of events in your life?

○ When I was laid off from a job and another better opportunity came along.
○ When a health problem I had was discovered just in time.
○ When I met my spouse.
○ When a special church service led me to accept Jesus as my Savior and Lord.
○ Other _____.

2. If the locusts are not literal, what might they represent? How might such a creature literally come to exist?

3. Once again, note the ways in which God is in control over all events and powers. Find examples in this passage.

4. The four angels who will kill a third of the entire human race "were prepared" precisely for that purpose at an exact time (v. 15). What does this say about God?

5. If the horses are not literal, what might they represent? Might there one day be a military weapon like this?

6. What is God's purpose in pouring out these woes upon mankind? How does this passage make you feel?

7. Why do the people not repent? What "demons" and "idols" are worshiped in our country today? How can you be sure to keep an attitude of repentance?

GOING DEEPER:

If your group has time and/or wants a challenge, go on to this question.

8. How is the torment of locusts more frightening than the "woes" of last week? How do you reconcile the image of the wrath of God with the image of God as merciful and compassionate?

Caring Time   15 Min.

APPLY THE LESSON AND PRAY FOR ONE ANOTHER

Worshiping God can be a double-edged sword: he promises to keep us in his divine protection, but sometimes that includes allowing us to suffer—whether to discipline us for sin or to build perseverance. Take some time now to examine your own life, and to reach out in support of those who need help.

1. Are there any of the items from verses 20 and 21 in your life at present? How do you need to repent?

2. How can you praise God this week for the things he has done in your life?

3. Are there things in your life now for which you need to trust that God will faithfully work out the timing? How can the group pray for your strength and endurance?

Next Week

Today we watched as two more trumpets blasted further woes upon the human race, woes that God is sending in hopes of bringing people to repentance. In the coming week, examine your own life for areas that God may want you to change, and be quick to repent if necessary. Next week we will meet another remarkable angel, this time with a tiny scroll in his hand.

Notes on Revelation 9:1–21

SUMMARY: The fifth plague (the first woe) is recounted in more detail than the first four. It involves the attack of fierce locusts that sting but do not kill. In Joel 2:1–11, it had been prophesied that a plague of locusts would precede the Day of the Lord.

9:1 *a star.* A heavenly figure with the power to unlock the underworld. *the abyss.* In the pictorial way in which the Bible speaks of the cosmos, there are said to be three levels—the heavens, the earth and the underworld (which is a huge, bottomless pit). It is the realm of the dead (Rom. 10:7); it is where the beast abides (11:7); it is the place of demons (Luke 8:31); it will be used as the prison of Satan during the Millennium (20:3); and in this case, it is the home of the demon locusts. The Abyss is connected to the surface of the earth via a shaft.

9:3 *locusts.* These are not actual locusts, but some sort of demonic entity. Their coming is similar to the plague of (real) locusts in Exodus 10:1–20. *scorpions.* A large spider-like poisonous creature, which has a stinger on the end of its tail.

9:4 Real locusts consume plants, trees and grass. These locusts lack that ability, attacking only humans. *God's seal.* God's wrath will not fall upon those who are his people; only upon those who worship the beast (16:2). This is not to say that God's people will be spared suffering and persecution—only that it will not be from God.

9:5 *five months.* The significance of this time period is not clear. It may refer to the life cycle of the locust (which is five months), or to the five-month period when an invasion of locusts is most likely. Probably it is merely intended to indicate that the suffering will be confined to a short period of time. The aim of these acts after all is not to torment but to bring about repentance.

9:7 The locusts looked like horses. In some cultures (e.g., in Arabia), the head of the locust is thought to look like the head of a horse. In Joel 2:4, the locusts are described as war horses. *crowns.* These symbolize, perhaps, the fact that the locusts have the power to succeed in their mission to tor-

ment humankind. *men's faces.* This may refer to their intelligence.

9:8 *hair like women's hair.* Perhaps a reference to the antennae of locusts, or to the hair on their legs or bodies. *lions' teeth.* Locusts are fierce in the way they destroy vegetation.

9:9 *iron breastplates.* The scales on the bodies of locusts are shaped like this. *the sound of their wings.* When locusts swarm into an area, they make a loud noise by the beating of their wings.

9:11 *their king.* This figure is unique with no parallel in biblical or other Jewish literature. *Abaddon.* A Hebrew word meaning "destruction." In the Old Testament, this word is used along with "Sheol" for the place of destruction and death (Job 26:6; 28:22; Prov. 15:11; 27:20). *Apollyon.* This Greek word is not the usual word used to translate Abaddon. It is a participle meaning "destroyer."

9:12 This refers back to 8:13. The first woe is passed. The second will be described in 9:13–21, when the sixth trumpet is sounded. The third woe will come when the seventh trumpet is sounded in 11:14–19.

9:13–21 The plague of the fifth trumpet brought pain and suffering; this plague brings death. The Old Testament parallel for such an invasion of horses is found in Ezekiel 38:12–16 (Isa. 5:26–30; Jer. 6:22–26).

9:13 *a voice.* This is either the collective voice of the martyrs whose prayers are upon the throne, crying out for vindication, or the voice of the angel who presented their prayers to God (8:3–4).

9:14 *the four angels.* Again, as with the seven trumpet-angels, this appears to be a definite group.

However, four angels such as these are nowhere mentioned in apocalyptic literature. *bound.* These are probably fallen angels, held in check so they could not exercise their evil intentions. Now they are released and they kill a third of mankind. How this killing takes place is not indicated. Probably they were commanders of the great army of horses. *the great river Euphrates.* The eastern boundary of the Promised Land (Gen. 15:18). Beyond it lived the enemies of the Jewish nation. The releasing of these hordes would probably conjure up images for John's readers of the dreaded Parthians.

9:17 *The horses.* The demon locusts in the previous plague are followed by demon horses in this plague. There is a difference. While the locusts had the power to torture, the horses have the power to kill. *breastplates.* This description could refer to the armor of the riders or to the armor of both riders and horses. Beyond this, little is said about the riders. The focus is on the terrifying horses. *fire, smoke, and sulfur.* Fire, smoke and sulfur (brimstone) of this sort are straight out of hell (14:10–11; 19:20; 21:8).

9:20–21 The intent of the plagues is revealed. It is not vengeance—it is to lead humanity to repentance. Despite the horror of the plagues, people still refuse to turn from their worship of demons and the lifestyle that such a commitment brings. *demons and idols.* They err in worshiping evil powers (demons) and dumb idols that have no life. In either case, this keeps them from worshiping the living God. In 1 Corinthians Paul makes an interesting point when he asserts that demons stand behind dumb idols. To worship idols is to give oneself over to the demonic (1 Cor. 10:18–21).

SESSION 11
The Angel and the Scroll
SCRIPTURE REVELATION 10:1–11

Last Week

In last week's session, we heard another series of trumpet blasts, sounding forth in judgment and warning on the people of the earth. We were reminded of the importance of repentance and turning from the sin in our life. This week John himself speaks face-to-face with another intimidating angel, who gives him a scroll and an extraordinary command. He tells John to eat it!

Ice-Breaker   15 Min.
CONNECT WITH YOUR GROUP

LEADER

Open with a word of prayer. Choose one, two or all three of the Ice-Breaker questions, depending on your group's needs.

Food is one of the true pleasures of life … most of the time. Sometimes the things we eat can disagree with us, and what follows may not be fun at all! Take turns sharing some of your experiences with culinary delights.

1. What is your favorite sweet?

- ○ Chocolate.
- ○ Ice cream.
- ○ Cake.
- ○ Candy bars.
- ○ Pie.
- ○ Hard candy.
- ○ Other _____.

2. Have you ever eaten something that tasted great but had an undesirable affect on you?

3. What book have you read that you just "devoured," not wanting to put it down?

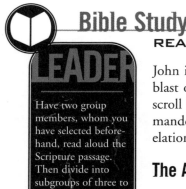

Bible Study 30 Min.

READ SCRIPTURE AND DISCUSS

John is now confronted with another angel, but this one does not blast out a trumpet of woe upon the earth. Instead, he has a tiny scroll in his hand, a scroll that is open and not sealed. John is commanded to take the scroll ... but not for reading pleasure. Read Revelation 10:1–11, and note what John is instructed to do.

The Angel and the Scroll

Reader One: 10 Then I saw another mighty angel coming down from heaven, surrounded by a cloud, with a rainbow over his head. His face was like the sun, his legs were like fiery pillars, ²and he had a little scroll opened in his hand. He put his right foot on the sea, his left on the land, ³and he cried out with a loud voice like a roaring lion. When he cried out, the seven thunders spoke with their voices. ⁴And when the seven thunders spoke, I was about to write. Then I heard a voice from heaven, saying,

Reader Two: "Seal up what the seven thunders said, and do not write it down!"

Reader One: ⁵Then the angel that I had seen standing on the sea and on the land raised his right hand to heaven. ⁶He swore an oath by the One who lives forever and ever, who created heaven and what is in it, the earth and what is in it, and the sea and what is in it:

Reader Two: "There will no longer be an interval of time, ⁷but in the days of the sound of the seventh angel, when he will blow his trumpet, then God's hidden plan will be completed, as He announced to His servants the prophets."

Reader One: ⁸Now the voice that I heard from heaven spoke to me again and said,

Reader Two: "Go, take the scroll that lies open in the hand of the angel who is standing on the sea and on the land."

Reader One: ⁹So I went to the angel and asked him to give me the little scroll. He said to me,

Reader Two: "Take and eat it; it will be bitter in your stomach, but it will be as sweet as honey in your mouth."

Reader One: ¹⁰Then I took the little scroll from the angel's hand and ate it. It was as sweet as honey in my mouth, but when I ate it, my stomach became bitter. ¹¹And I was told,

Reader Two: "You must prophesy again about many peoples, nations, languages, and kings."

Revelation 10:1–11

QUESTIONS FOR INTERACTION

LEADER

Refer to the Summary and Study Notes at the end of this session as needed. If 30 minutes is not enough time to answer all of the questions in this section, conclude the Bible Study by answering questions 6 and 7.

1. What do you imagine when you think of an angel?

   ○ A being that watches over me and keeps me safe.
   ○ A baby with wings.
   ○ A mighty archangel that battles evil forces.
   ○ A perfect being that always does the will of God.
   ○ Other _____.

2. Consider the description of the angel in this passage. What does each element (rainbow, fiery pillars, etc.) represent? How is he like the God he serves?

3. Why does the angel stand with one foot upon the sea and one upon the land?

4. Why is the scroll "sweet as honey" in John's mouth, yet bitter in his stomach (v. 10)? Has God's Word ever affected you that way?

5. Why does John eat the scroll instead of reading it? What does this tell us about our own approach to God's Word?

6. Why must John prophesy about "many peoples, nations, languages, and kings" (v. 11)? To whom is God calling you to share the Gospel?

7. God's plan has long been "hidden," but the time is coming soon when it will be completed and revealed. How does this encourage you in your daily walk with the Lord?

GOING DEEPER:

If your group has time and/or wants a challenge, go on to this question.

8. John asks the angel to hand him the scroll, but he is told repeatedly to *take* it. Why is this distinction important? What does it tell us about our own approach to God's Word?

♥ Caring Time   15 Min.

LEADER

Conclude the prayer time by asking God for guidance in determining the future mission and outreach of this group.

God's Word is alive and powerful. At times it can be sweet as honey; at other times, it can turn our stomach. Our reaction to the Word depends, not on the Word itself, but on how willing we are to receive it. Gather around each other now in this time of sharing and prayer.

1. How have you seen the Holy Spirit at work in your life this past week?

2. Is God's Word still "sweet as honey" in your mouth? If not, how can the group help you regain that sweetness?

3. What can this group do to reach out to "many peoples, nations, languages"?

🌐 Next Week

Today we were confronted by an angel who presented us with God's Word, represented by an open scroll and freely available to anyone who will take it. In the coming week, take the Word that God makes so available, spending time in personal reading and meditation. If it lacks sweetness, ask God to teach you how to regain the sweetness of your salvation. Next week we will meet two mysterious and powerful men who testify to the glory of God.

Notes on Revelation 10:1–11

SUMMARY: John inserts an extended interlude between the sixth and seventh trumpets, just as he did between the sixth and seventh seals. This interlude, like the other, has two parts to it. In part one, he relates the account of the mighty angel and the little scroll (10:1–11). In part two, he tells about measuring the temple and the two witnesses (11:1–14).

10:1 The description of this angel is so similar to that of Christ in chapter 1 that some commentators have identified him as such. However, in verse 6 he shows himself to be a genuine angel by swearing by "the One who lives forever and ever." *coming down from heaven.* In 4:1 John was caught up to heaven, but now, it seems, he is back on earth and the angel descends to him. This is yet another example of the fluid language used in apocalyptic literature. This book must not be read as if it were an ordered, linear account to be interpreted like straight narrative. *surrounded by a cloud.* Angels were described as ascending and descending on clouds (Ps. 104:3; Dan. 7:13; Acts 1:9), but this one is clothed in a cloud. *rainbow.* This can be understood as a kind of crown or as the reflection of his brilliance ("his face was like the sun") through the clouds.

10:2 *a little scroll.* This is an unusual word, used nowhere else in Greek literature prior to this time. John probably coined it himself. Unlike the scroll of 5:1, which was a book, this scroll was more akin to a booklet. *opened.* Unlike the other scroll, the contents of this one were not hidden.

10:3 *the seven thunders.* No information is given as to the nature of these thunders.

10:4 John understood what the seven thunders communicated but he is told not to record them. What these thunders convey is, of course, unknown. But in each of the three other instances in Revelation where there is thunder, it is the precursor to judgment (8:5; 11:19; 16:18).

10:5 With the scroll in his left hand, the angel proceeds to lift his right hand toward heaven as he prepares to take an oath (Deut. 32:40; Dan. 12:7).

10:6 What he swears is that there will be no more delay before the coming of the end.

10:7 *in the days of.* The sounding of the seventh trumpet is not a single act but a period of time. As will emerge, it includes the events of the seven bowls (16:1–21).

10:8 *the voice.* The same voice that forbade John to record the words of the seven thunders (v. 4) now tells him to take the scroll. *the angel who is standing on the sea and on the land.* For the third time the tremendous size of this angel is emphasized. His coming has something to do with all of the earth (vv. 2,5).

10:9 *Take and eat it.* Ezekiel was commanded to do the very same thing. (In Ezek. 2:9–3:3, Ezekiel is told to ingest the Word of God, i.e. to assimilate it into his very being.) This was a symbol of his commission to receive the Word of God and then proclaim it. In the same way, John is recommissioned to speak God's prophetic Word in this end time (1:19).

10:10 *bitter/sweet.* This message is both bitter (Ps. 19:8–10; 119:103; Ezek. 3:3) and it is sweet (Isa. 66:16; Jer. 25:31; Luke 19:41–44). To be called to be a prophet is a mixed blessing.

10:11 *prophesy again.* John has already given the prophecy of the seven seals and the six trumpets. He is to continue to prophesy as the end approaches. *about many peoples.* His message concerns the whole world, not just the church or Israel or any other single nation.

The Two Witnesses
SCRIPTURE REVELATION 11:1–19

Last Week

In last week's session, we watched as John ate the tiny scroll from the hand of the angel—tasting sweet in his mouth but turning bitter in his stomach. We were encouraged to take a new look at God's Word and appreciate all it has to offer. This week we will encounter two men who experience more bitterness in life than just something they ate— they will give their very lives in service to God and the Gospel.

Ice-Breaker   15 Min.
CONNECT WITH YOUR GROUP

LEADER

Open with a word of prayer, and then have your group discuss one, two or all three of the Ice-Breaker questions, depending on your group's needs.

Water is something we take for granted when we have it, but miss quickly when it's gone. In today's Scripture passage, the two witnesses have the power to "close the sky." Share some of your experiences with times of plentiful water and drought.

1. What memories do you have of swimming as a child?

2. Where would you least like to live—an area prone to earthquakes, hurricanes or floods, and why?

3. Have you ever lived through a drought? How long did it last? How did it affect you?

Bible Study

READ SCRIPTURE AND DISCUSS

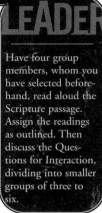

Have four group members, whom you have selected beforehand, read aloud the Scripture passage. Assign the readings as outlined. Then discuss the Questions for Interaction, dividing into smaller groups of three to six.

John is commanded to measure the temple and to count those in it, excluding those outside of the sanctuary. Suddenly, we are confronted by two men, "witnesses" to the glory and justice of God. This is a difficult passage (as are many in Revelation), but we can always learn something about God and what he expects of us by studying it. Read Revelation 11:1–19, and note the role that worship plays once again.

The Two Witnesses

Reader One: 11 Then I was given a measuring reed like a rod, with these words: "Go and measure God's sanctuary and the altar, and count those who worship there. ²But exclude the courtyard outside the sanctuary. Don't measure it, because it is given to the nations, and they will trample the holy city for 42 months. ³I will empower my two witnesses, and they will prophesy for 1,260 days, dressed in sackcloth." ⁴These are the two olive trees and the two lampstands that stand before the Lord of the earth. ⁵If anyone wants to harm them, fire comes from their mouths and consumes their enemies; if anyone wants to harm them, he must be killed in this way. ⁶These men have the power to close the sky so that it does not rain during the days of their prophecy. They also have power over the waters to turn them into blood, and to strike the earth with any plague whenever they want.

Reader Two: ⁷When they finish their testimony, the beast that comes up out of the abyss will make war with them, conquer them, and kill them. ⁸Their dead bodies will lie in the public square of the great city, which is called, prophetically, Sodom and Egypt, where also their Lord was crucified. ⁹And representatives from the peoples, tribes, languages, and nations will view their bodies for three and a half days and not permit their bodies to be put into a tomb. ¹⁰Those who live on the earth will gloat over them and celebrate and send gifts to one another, because these two prophets tormented those who live on the earth.

Reader Three: ¹¹But after the three and a half days, the breath of life from God entered them, and they stood on their feet. So great fear fell on those who saw them. ¹²Then they heard a loud voice from heaven saying to them, "Come up here." They went up to heaven in a cloud, while their enemies watched them. ¹³At that moment a violent earthquake took place, a tenth of the city fell, and 7,000 people were killed in the earthquake. The survivors were terrified and gave glory to the God of heaven. ¹⁴The second woe has passed. Take note: the third woe is coming quickly!

Reader Four: [15]The seventh angel blew his trumpet, and there were loud voices in heaven saying:

> The kingdom of the world has become the kingdom
> of our Lord and of His Messiah,
> and He will reign forever and ever!

[16]The 24 elders, who were seated before God on their thrones, fell on their faces and worshiped God, [17]saying:

> We thank You, Lord God, the Almighty, who is and who was,
> because You have taken Your great power and have begun to reign.
> [18]The nations were angry, but Your wrath has come.
> The time has come for the dead to be judged,
> and to give the reward to Your servants the prophets,
> to the saints, and to those who fear Your name, both small and great,
> and the time has come to destroy those who destroy the earth.

[19]God's sanctuary in heaven was opened, and the ark of His covenant appeared in His sanctuary. There were lightnings, rumblings, thunders, an earthquake, and severe hail.

Revelation 11:1–19

QUESTIONS FOR INTERACTION

LEADER

Refer to the Summary and Study Notes at the end of this session as needed. If 30 minutes is not enough time to answer all of the questions in this section, conclude the Bible Study by answering question 7.

1. When do you feel that you especially need the protection of God?

- ○ When I'm in a tempting situation.
- ○ When I'm driving or flying.
- ○ When I'm having health problems.
- ○ Other _____.

2. The implication of John's measuring in verses 1 and 2 seems to be that those measured will be protected by God. Who receives this protection?

3. Why does God command John to "exclude the courtyard outside the sanctuary" (v. 2)? What is the significance that the "nations" are "outside the sanctuary"?

4. If these two witnesses are not two literal individuals, who or what might they represent? What would their powers represent?

5. How do the witnesses torment those who live on earth? What is the real cause of their torment?

6. Why would the world "gloat over" the downfall of the witnesses (v. 10)? Have you seen this happen in today's world?

7. What do you learn in this passage about what it means to be a witness? What has been toughest for you about living out your faith at work, school or home?

GOING DEEPER:

If your group has time and/or wants a challenge, go on to this question.

8. Moses and Elijah were two real men who actually performed miracles similar to those of the two witnesses (Ex. 7–11; 1 Kin. 17–19). If these two witnesses are literal people, who might they be? What would their powers be?

Caring Time   15 Min.

APPLY THE LESSON AND PRAY FOR ONE ANOTHER

LEADER

Following the Caring Time, discuss with your group how they would like to celebrate the last session next week. Also, discuss the possibility of splitting into two groups or continuing together with another study (perhaps book 2 of the study of Revelation).

Every believer in Christ is a "witness" to the people around us, presenting the power and majesty of God in our own lives. Come together now and encourage one another to go out and spread the Gospel to all in need.

1. What can you do in the coming week to encourage a fellow group member in being an effective witness for Christ?

2. How effective a witness are you to the world around you? Are you clothed in sackcloth or in fine clothes?

3. Is there a brother or sister in your church or community who has fallen? How can you help to restore him or her?

Next Week

This week we met two striking men who bear witness to the power and majesty of God. In the coming week, consider what kind of witness your own life brings to the people around you, and ask the Lord to teach you to be a dramatic example of his power. Next week we will meet some even more vivid characters—a huge red dragon and the pregnant woman he wants to devour.

Notes on Revelation 11:1–19

SUMMARY: The measuring of the temple in Jerusalem and the account of the two witnesses is the second part of the interlude between the sixth and seventh trumpets. This is an exceedingly difficult section to interpret. Four main lines of interpretation have been developed. First, many consider this to be an earlier piece of prophecy, written before 70 A.D., which tells of the literal, historical destruction of the temple by the Romans. However, it seems unlikely that John would have included a piece of apocalyptic writing from an earlier time, especially since some details had not been fulfilled (e.g., the inner courtyard [vv. 1–2] was not preserved from destruction by the Romans). Second, others think this is a prophecy that is to be interpreted literally; namely, that at the end of the age the temple will be restored and will be the site of the struggle between restored Jews and the beast. Third, some feel this is a prediction of the preservation of the Jewish people and their final salvation. Fourth, still others feel this is a prophecy about the fate of the witnessing church during its final period of opposition and persecution, akin to the sealing of the church described in 7:1–8.

11:1 *I.* John, who has been a passive spectator up to 10:8 (when he is given the scroll to eat), is asked to continue to be an active participant in the vision. *measure.* To measure is not simply to note the dimensions of the area. It is to set aside a place, either for destruction or for preservation (2 Kin. 21:13; Isa. 34:11; Ezek. 40–43; Zech. 2:1–5). In this case, the area that John measures is to be preserved. *sanctuary.* The Greek word refers to the temple building itself and not the outer courtyard. The temple itself consisted of a building at the center (containing the Most Holy Place), bordered by the court of the priests, the court of Israel and the court of the women. These courts were where the people of Israel assembled. This temple complex was surrounded by a huge outer court where Gentiles were allowed to come. What John is asked to measure is the inner, Jewish area.

11:2 *42 months.* Three and a half years, the length of time evil is allowed to dominate (12:6,14; 13:5; Dan. 7:25). Many people believe that the original reference in Daniel is probably to the period of time that the Jews suffered under the Syrian king Antiochus Epiphanes in 167–164 B.C.

11:3 *two witnesses.* It seems clear that these two men are modeled after Moses and Elijah (Ex. 7:14–18; 1 Kin. 17:1; 2 Kin. 1:10–12; Mal. 4:5; Mark 9:4). In this context, they may be two individuals who preach repentance to Israel; or they may be symbols of the witnessing church. During the time of domination of evil, witness to God continues. *1,260 days.* Three and a half years = 42 months = 1,260 days (a solar month had 30 days). *sackcloth.* A coarse, dark cloth which signified mourning; it was the clothing often worn by prophets (Isa. 20:2; Zech. 13:4).

11:7 *the beast.* This is the first time that this figure appears. He will become the major threat to the church in the last days (ch. 13; 17). His origins are clear: he is a demon out of the Abyss.

11:10–12 A holiday is declared now that those who tormented their consciences are dead. But the resurrection of the witnesses cuts short the rejoicing (Ezek. 37). This is followed by the open, visible ascension into heaven of the two witnesses (2 Kin. 2:11).

11:13 This is followed by a devastating earthquake that levels a tenth of the city (Ezek. 38:19–20). *gave glory to the God of heaven.* As other texts indicate, this is probably not true repentance (13:3–4) but rather an astonished acknowledgment of the power of God in response to the amazing resurrection of the witnesses.

11:15 The rule of the world is now firmly and fully in the hands of God the Father and God the Son. This anticipates what will happen following the events described in the next chapters. *He will reign for ever and ever.* No more will Satan or evil disturb reality. Once his kingdom is established in fullness, God will reign from then on, uninterrupted.

11:18 *The nations were angry.* Before God's kingdom could come, power had to be taken away from those who were hostile to God (Ps. 2). *Your wrath has come.* So God came in judgment (14:10–11; 16:15–21; 20:8–9). *saints.* Those who are God's people from all ages. *destroy those who destroy the earth.* Humanity was created to be the steward of the earth (Gen. 1:26), but the result of human sin has led even creation itself to groan (Rom. 8:19–22). God's final judgment will be a time when judgment is directed against those who have worked against God and the good of his creation.

11:19 *God's sanctuary in heaven was opened.* At the time of Jesus' death, the curtain in the temple in Jerusalem was torn in two, signifying that now men and women have free access to God (Matt. 27:51; Heb. 10:19–21). That access, which was until this time spiritual, is now given concrete form. This opening up of the temple (along with the other events in vv. 15b–19) will, in fact, occur in chapters 21–22. But here, in this vision that speaks of the future as if it were the present, the outcome of the end times is declared. The culmination of John's vision of seven trumpets is this insight into the heavenly holy place where God dwells. *the ark of His covenant.* In the Old Testament the Ark of the Covenant was a wooden chest which stood in the Holy of Holies and symbolized the presence of God. The ark was lost during one of the conflicts in Israel, but here it is restored as an indication of the fulfillment of the covenants God made with his people. *lightnings, rumblings, thunders, an earthquake, and severe hail.* These signify the awesome presence of God.

SESSION 13
The Dragon and the Woman
SCRIPTURE REVELATION 12:1–18

Last Week

Last week we met two dramatic characters—witnesses who gave their lives for the Gospel, only to be resurrected and snatched into heaven while the whole world watched. We were reminded that we also need to be bold and powerful witnesses for Christ. This week we will have another vivid story unfold, as we watch a huge dragon sweep the stars out of the sky with his tail and try to devour a pregnant woman. Fortunately, he is not powerful enough to defeat the forces of heaven, and he is cast down. Unfortunately, he lands on earth.

Ice-Breaker   15 Min.

CONNECT WITH YOUR GROUP

LEADER

Begin this final session with a word of prayer and thanksgiving for this time together. Choose one or two Ice-Breaker questions to discuss.

Hiking out into the wilderness can be a real adventure, especially if one encounters dangerous beasts there. Of course, one does not always need to go far to find dangerous beasts—some of our fellow humans can provide that excitement. Take turns sharing some of your experiences with dangerous people and places.

1. What is your favorite story about dragons?

- ○ *The Tales of King Arthur.*
- ○ *The Hobbit.*
- ○ *The Dragon Slayer.*
- ○ *Voyage of the Dawn Treader.*
- ○ Other _____.

2. Who was the "big bully" who terrorized you as a child? Where is that person now?

3. What is the longest camping trip you've ever taken? What "wilderness" did you explore?

If last week's story was not dramatic enough, just hang on. This week we will meet a fiery red dragon who takes on the powers of heaven. He loses, and in his rage he sweeps stars out of the sky with his tail on his way down. Unfortunately for us, he lands here on earth. Read Revelation 12:1–18, and note how the angels help once again.

The Dragon and the Woman

Reader One: 12 A great sign appeared in heaven: a woman clothed with the sun, with the moon under her feet, and a crown of 12 stars on her head. ²She was pregnant and cried out in labor and agony to give birth. ³Then another sign appeared in heaven: There was a great fiery red dragon having seven heads and 10 horns, and on his heads were seven diadems. ⁴His tail swept away a third of the stars in heaven and hurled them to the earth. And the dragon stood in front of the woman who was about to give birth, so that when she did give birth he might devour her child. ⁵But she gave birth to a Son – a male who is going to shepherd all nations with an iron scepter – and her child was caught up to God and to His throne. ⁶The woman fled into the wilderness, where she had a place prepared by God, to be fed there for 1,260 days.

Reader Two: ⁷Then war broke out in heaven: Michael and his angels fought against the dragon. The dragon and his angels also fought, ⁸but he could not prevail, and there was no place for them in heaven any longer. ⁹So the great dragon was thrown out – the ancient serpent, who is called the Devil and Satan, the one who deceives the whole world. He was thrown to earth, and his angels with him.

Reader Three: ¹⁰Then I heard a loud voice in heaven say:
　The salvation and the power and the kingdom of our God
　and the authority of His Messiah have now come,
　because the accuser of our brothers has been thrown out:
　the one who accuses them before our God day and night.
¹¹They conquered him by the blood of the Lamb
　and by the word of their testimony,
　for they did not love their lives in the face of death.
¹²Therefore rejoice, O heavens, and you who dwell in them!
　Woe to the earth and the sea,
　for the Devil has come down to you with great fury,
　because he knows he has a short time.

Reader Four: ¹³When the dragon saw that he had been thrown to earth, he persecuted the woman who gave birth to the male. ¹⁴The woman was given two wings of a great eagle, so that she could fly from the serpent's presence to her place in the wilderness, where she was fed for a time, times, and half a time. ¹⁵From his mouth the serpent spewed water like a river after the woman, to sweep her away in a torrent. ¹⁶But the earth helped the woman: the earth opened its mouth and swallowed up the river that the dragon had spewed from his mouth. ¹⁷So the dragon was furious with the woman and left to wage war against the rest of her offspring – those who keep the commandments of God and have the testimony about Jesus. ¹⁸He stood on the sand of the sea.

Revelation 12:1–18

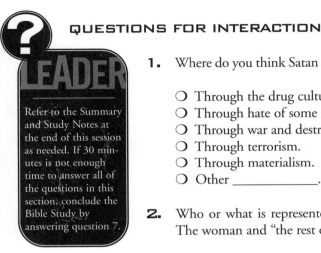

QUESTIONS FOR INTERACTION

1. Where do you think Satan is working hardest in the world today?

○ Through the drug culture.
○ Through hate of some religions toward Christianity.
○ Through war and destruction.
○ Through terrorism.
○ Through materialism.
○ Other _____.

Refer to the Summary and Study Notes at the end of this session as needed. If 30 minutes is not enough time to answer all of the questions in this section, conclude the Bible Study by answering question 7.

2. Who or what is represented by the dragon? The woman's son? The woman and "the rest of her offspring" (v. 17)?

3. Satan "could not prevail" in his war in heaven, but "was thrown out" (v. 9). The bad news is that he now wages war here on earth. What is the good news?

4. Verse 11 says that Satan has been "conquered"—in the past tense. He is already defeated. How has this been accomplished, according to this passage? How is this both bad news and good news for us?

5. Why is the Devil in a "great fury" (v. 12)? How is this knowledge encouraging to us?

6. When has Satan seemed very real to you? How did you overcome him?

7. What spiritual battle have you faced? Did you view it as a spiritual battle at the time? What do you need to do to become stronger for spiritual battle?

GOING DEEPER:

If your group has time and/or wants a challenge, go on to this question.

8. Examine this passage for the many ways in which God has all things under his control, as part of his plan. How does he intervene directly to help his people? How does he use other beings or forces to accomplish his will?

Caring Time   15 Min.

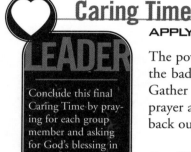

APPLY THE LESSON AND PRAY FOR ONE ANOTHER

LEADER

Conclude this final Caring Time by praying for each group member and asking for God's blessing in any plans to start a new group or continue to study together.

The power of Satan is very real and very literal in our world. That's the bad news; the good news is that he has already been defeated. Gather around each other now in this final time of sharing and prayer and encourage one another to have faith and hope as you go back out into the world.

1. What was your serendipity (unexpected blessing) during this course?

2. How can the knowledge that Satan is already conquered help you this week in doing battle with him?

3. How would you like the group to continue to pray for you?

Next Week

This week we were given a glimpse of the day that Satan was cast out of heaven, and we were allowed to understand why he is so angry— he has already lost the battle, and he knows that his time is short. In the coming week, ask the Lord to protect you from the enemy of our souls, and thank God for the fact that he and all his powers are already undone. If your group has decided to continue the study of Revelation with Book 2, in the next session we will meet Satan's henchmen, the two beasts.

SUMMARY: For the third time John inserts an interlude into his account. Between the account of the seven trumpets and the account of the seven bowls, he tells the story of the dragon and the woman (12:1–13:1a), the vision of the two great beasts (13:1b–18), and the vision of the Lamb on Mount Zion (14:1–20). John describes, using a variety of symbols, the war in heaven between the forces of God and the forces of Satan. This explains why it is that the people of God have faced suffering and persecution down through the ages (John 16:33; Acts 14:22). It explains the intensification of the battle between good and evil during the Great Tribulation (Matt. 24:21). It also assures believers that the outcome of the battle is not in question. God has already won and that fact will soon be displayed for all to see.

12:1 *a woman.* The first participant in this heavenly drama is introduced: the radiant woman who represents the idealized Israel, the mother of the people of God (Isa. 54:1; 66:7–8; Gal. 4:26). The details of her dress indicate her magnificence. *a crown of 12 stars.* Perhaps this symbolizes the 12 tribes (Gen. 37:9).

12:2 *pregnant.* She is the mother of the Messiah (v. 5; Isa. 66:7–8; Mic. 5:3) and also the church (v. 17).

12:3 *fiery red dragon.* The second participant comes on stage: the great dragon who is Satan (v. 9). The dragon/serpent is seen as the embodiment of evil in the Old Testament (Ps. 74:14; Isa. 27:1; 51:9). *heads.* His seven heads indicate great intelligence *10 horns.* See Daniel 7:7. *seven diadems.* Seven is the number of completeness; a crown is the sign of power. Satan is a figure of enormous power …

12:4 *swept away a third of the stars.* This is another sign of his enormous power and may reflect his conquest of a large number of angelic beings. *devour her child.* The purpose of Satan is revealed: he wants to destroy the Messiah.

12:5 *a male.* The third participant appears. The language used to describe him clearly indicates that he is the Messiah (2:27; 19:15; Ps. 2:9). *caught up to God.* No specific events in the life of Christ are conveyed in the descriptions in this verse (this is not his actual birth or Herod's attempt to destroy him or his ascension, though all these events show the truth of this account). All this takes place in the heavens. The point of the verse is that he escapes the dragon.

12:6 Frustrated in its attempt to devour the child, the dragon turns on the mother. However, she is protected by God, as the church on earth will be during the three and one half years when the dragon is loose on earth. *wilderness.* This is not a wasteland but a place of refuge (as it often was for the children of Israel). *1,260 days.* This is the period of time that evil is allowed to do its work upon earth.

12:7 *Michael.* See Daniel 12:1.

12:9 *the ancient serpent.* An allusion to Genesis 3:1–5. *the Devil.* Literally, *diabolos,* a Greek term for Satan meaning "accuser," "adversary," or "slanderer" (Zech. 3:1–2; 1 Peter 5:8). *Satan.* A Hebrew term meaning "accuser" (Job 1:6).

12:10 This announcement, like that in 11:15, states in the present what will be accomplished in the future.

12:11 The source of Satan's defeat is now announced: it came through the death of Jesus on the cross. That defeat continues to be manifested by the word of testimony of those who were martyrs—those who followed in Christ's footsteps and were faithful unto death.

12:12 The defeat of Satan has two results. There is rejoicing in heaven among those who are of

God, but there is woe on earth because Satan will now exercise his power there. *woe to the earth.* Some say that this is the third woe announced in 8:13.

12:14 She escapes by means of a pair of eagle wings that she is given (Deut. 32:10–11; Isa. 40:31). Once again, the assurance is given to the church that it will be preserved. *a time, times, and half a time.* One year plus two years plus a half a year. This phrase is taken from Daniel 7:25, and is the same time period as three and a half years = 42 months = 1,260 days.

12:17 The woman has already given birth to the Messiah and he has escaped Satan (v. 5). Now Satan turns his wrath on her other children (who, in this metaphor, are God's people). They already have victory over Satan (v. 10), but Satan can still harm them. This is John's word of encouragement to the church in his time: Satan, indeed, may persecute you, but in reality he has already been defeated.

Personal Notes

Personal Notes

Personal Notes

Personal Notes

Personal Notes

Personal Notes

Personal Notes

Personal Notes